Forward

For as much as The Perfect Pointe Book has been around in various formats over the last 2 years, the fact it is finally in a physical form and available from a highly respected company like BLOCH really does say a lot about how far we have come with our vision.

I have been blessed to have made so many connections over the last few years through the creation of The Perfect Pointe Book and I can see now there is no stopping this movement of healthy educated and talented dancers. My greatest thanks go to BLOCH for their faith and foresight in aligning with myself and my company and giving us the wonderful privilege of being represented in their store and under their brand. It is truly an exciting time when a dancewear retailer is so dedicated and focused on helping educate their clients and I am honored to collaborate on this project with them.

Special thanks must go to Sandie, Sallyanne and Karen from the York St store in Sydney, Australia for their generosity in providing all of the dancewear used in our photographs, as well as their constant support of the work I do to educate young dancers. Having spent many hours in conversation with Sandie, Sallyanne and Karen, I know that they share a similar vision in caring for all our young dancers and empowering all of them with great information and awesome products that help protect dancers from the rigors of the trade.

I look forward to many more exciting projects with the team at Bloch in the coming months and years.

Disclaimer

The exercises given in this book are intended for use by girls who have been studying ballet for several years under the guidance of a qualified teacher. This is not a substitute for regular ballet lessons, but is designed to be an extra training program to enable girls to prepare their feet for pointe work. Completing the tests does not necessarily mean that you are safe to go onto pointe. The information given here is not a substitute for medical advice. It is to provide extra information to the many dance students who may not have access to individual specialized care. You should always get approval from your teacher, and preferably an assessment by a physiotherapist (physical therapist) who specializes in dancers, before progressing onto pointe.

None of these exercises should cause any pain or discomfort (beyond that of muscles working!) If you are unsure about any pain you are feeling, please discontinue the exercise and consult your teacher. Sensible use of the tests and exercises in this book should result in rapid gains in strength and control in the feet. The author will not accept responsibility for any injury sustained while performing these exercises. They are all safe if the guidelines and detailed instructions are adhered to. If you are concerned about any of the exercises and their suitability for you, please consult your dance teacher for further advice.

Table of Contents

Introduction

It's Time for Toe Shoes!

There comes a time when every student that does ballet starts thinking about getting ready for pointe work. It is such an exciting time and almost everyone is keen to get onto their toes as soon as possible. Most of us have dreamt of drifting beautifully across a stage on our toes since our very first ballet class, and the closer the time comes, the harder it gets to wait!

So... when is the right time???

There is no one age or grade level that is right for everyone to jump into pointe shoes. Some girls are ready at eleven, some at fourteen, and some feet are just not made for pointe work. It depends more on how strong and well placed you are. There are however, lots of ways to help prepare your feet and body for the demands of pointe work, and sometimes you can even surprise your teachers! Even if one foot is a little bit stiff to start with, by doing the right exercises and stretches, you might be ready to go up faster than you think.

By strengthening your feet before you begin pointe work, you may also avoid developing the bad habits that many dancers get when they start too early. It is much easier to learn good habits from the beginning than to unlearn bad ones! The more control you have over your toes, the easier pointe work is! You should ALWAYS check with a specialized Dance Physiotherapist (Physical Therapist) or an experienced teacher before starting pointe work. They will be able to check how your feet move, look at the bony shape of the feet, and check the flexibility and control in the rest of your body. However, by trying the tests and practicing the special exercises in this book you can prepare for this check up, and make starting en pointe much easier and more comfortable!

While you are still growing (often until you are about sixteen), there are soft parts in most of your bones where they grow longer (growth plates). There are lots of little bones in your feet, and if you are not strong enough in the feet when you start pointe, you may damage these growth plates. It is also very important to have very strong turnout muscles, as it is impossible to cheat turnout en pointe! You should be doing at least three ballet classes a week for at least a year before going onto pointe to build up strength in all the right places.

So... test yourself! See how strong you are. Test your friends (if you want to let them in on your secret that is!) Try the exercises and feel your dancing improve! Remember, there should be no pain with any of the exercises, although you may feel some muscles that you have never used before!

If you have any pain, talk to your teacher, or log onto 'The Ballet Blog' at www.theballetblog.com to get regular updates on tips for training and to ask us any questions you may have.

Most of all enjoy your dancing, fill it with love and the world will see it!

About This Book

This book was first designed to help girls teach themselves how to achieve the strength needed to proceed onto pointe work. However, this book will help all dancers, whether you are a beginner or have been dancing en pointe for years. Even if you are not going to go onto pointe for a few years, the earlier you start learning what moves what and what should stay where, the better!

After years of doing pre-pointe assessments and constantly seeing the same issues, it was obvious to me that there needed to be a way that girls could prepare for their actual assessment. Far too many students try to go onto pointe when their feet and bodies are just not ready. Teachers work hard in class to encourage everyone to work with good technique, however, as everybody and every foot is different, it is very difficult to give each person the individual exercises that they need when working in a group.

This book lets you work out your own special areas that need attention, which may be quite different to your friends' weaknesses. It is designed to be simple to follow, and to help you constantly improve your foot control and strength.

Along the way, there are also some little anatomy lessons, so that you can start to learn exactly what muscles you should be using! It is fun to imagine what is going on under your skin, and the pictures make it very easy.

How to Use This Book

I know this all looks a bit scary to start with... but it really is not that bad! To make this as easy as possible to follow, we have broken all the tests and exercises down into four stages, which focus on different areas that you need to strengthen before you go en pointe.

There is a two week program to do for each stage. There are two or three tests to do on the first day, and a check-list for you to make sure you are completing the exercises correctly. If there are parts of a test you find hard or can't control, make a cross in the table on the appropriate worksheet (in the workbook at the back of this book). You might like to print off a few spare copies of the workbook sheets and keep them in a special folder so you can repeat the program a few times.

After completing the two week program for that stage you can retest yourself and see just how much you have improved! If you can do the test really well, it is time to move onto the next stage.

Test	Weakness	Day 1	Day 13
Demi-Pointe Range Test	Reduced demi-pointe	X	X
	Reduced pointe range	X	
	Toes clawing	X	
	Pain behind the ankle		

Now, we can't all be perfect when we start everything, so chances are you will have a little trouble ticking off all the things on each of the check-lists. It's a good idea to get a friend to watch you so that you aren't looking at your feet the whole time! If no one else is around, use a mirror to check your form. There are pictures demonstrating all the bad things as well, so don't worry if you don't recognize some of the words!

For example, the first two weeks is all about making sure you have enough movement in your feet. Find the right table for that stage in 'The Workbook' and make a cross next to anything you do incorrectly in each test. Then, go back to that chart at the end of the two weeks and see what has changed. If the tests are still a little tricky after two weeks of doing the exercises it is okay to stick with that stage a little longer until you really get it right. The better you are at each stage the better you will be en pointe!

Each stage works on a different area and the exercises increase in difficulty as you go on. In the later stages, there are two days a week that take you back to exercises you did in the beginning, to make sure your feet remember how to do them!

These are all great exercises to continue with when you get onto pointe. There is an ongoing program at the end that you can do a couple of times a week to keep making your feet and body stronger and stronger!

Do the first day of a new stage on a day when you have a little more time (Sundays are usually good). Go through all the exercises for that stage slowly with the instructions, so that when you practice them during the week, they are easy to remember.

Once you have successfully completed all the stages and can perform all the tests really well, with your teacher's approval, it may be time to be assessed more professionally. Remember that there may be other things that need attention before you do go onto pointe, but you will be so much more prepared than most of the other students who go for an assessment!

Basic Tips For Doing The Exercises

Record Your Progress

Use the sheets in the workbook to mark off which exercises you have done each day. It does not really matter when in the day you do them, but if you are a bit warm (after class, or after a walk), you may improve on the stretches a little more. However, if you can do the exercises in the mornings, you will be much more aware of the muscles for the rest of the day and will use the mobility that you have gained to help improve your flexibility further. Try and do the exercises the same time every day, so that you get into a routine. If you can get up early before school, this is great, as long as you have time to concentrate! Some people find it better just before dinner, or before bed.

Frequency

Try and do the small foot muscle exercises as often as possible. You can do them while still in your shoes at school, while waiting for the bus, in the bath; wherever and whenever you like! Do not do the strengthening exercises such as the rises or other exercises more than once a day. You need some recovery time in between sets especially when you are trying to increase strength. If the muscle is getting too sore from being worked more than it is used to, rest it for two days, focusing on gentle stretches instead. Then begin the exercise again, with less repetitions and only every second day. Gradually build up the intensity again.

Be Specific!

It is always important to do the right exercises. This sounds simple, but we are all really good at practicing the exercises we know we are good at! It is much harder to spend time doing things that we find difficult. When you are dancing however, having balance in opposite muscle groups is very important. Use the tests (and the explanations of common weaknesses) to see where you are weak and then focus on the exercises that strengthen those specific muscles. This way, you will notice improvements really quickly, and be much stronger all over.

Attention

Remember that you do need to concentrate on these exercises! Half of the strengthening you will achieve is by learning how to tell the nerves how to switch the right muscles on. The more you can concentrate on what you are feeling in your body when you are doing the exercises the better! As you practice, this will become easier and easier, which is the whole idea. When it becomes natural to use all the right muscles, you won't need to try so hard to use them, and can use more attention on dancing beautifully!

Quality

Always remember that it is the quality (how well you do the exercises) that matters, not the quantity (how many you do), although if you can do both, it is even better! It is silly to practice exercises that you cannot do properly over and over again, as your body will learn the incorrect technique. We are trying to teach the body perfect alignment, so that it becomes second nature when you dance. For this reason we have broken down even the most basic steps into different parts. This means that you can train the section of the exercise that you are weak at separately, then practice the full exercise again with much better form.

Consistency

To retrain your body you need to stick at it. The muscles will take time to strengthen, so you can't just do the exercises once or twice and expect miracles to happen. That said however, I have had many dance teachers thank me for the "miracles" that I have worked with their dancers feet. So 'miracles' can, and do happen, but usually through lots of focused work! Focus on the stage you are working on and do all the exercises for that area for at least two weeks. Actually building bigger muscle fibers can take six to twelve weeks of training, but improvements in technique from learning which muscles to use can happen much more quickly, and sometimes immediately!

Basic Positions for Doing the Exercises
What is "Neutral Spine"?

For most of the exercises, the instructions tell you to keep a "neutral spine". Some of you may know what this is, but many may not. There should actually be three small curves in your back when you are standing properly. You can change the shape of the curves in your back by tilting your hips forward and back, and by using different muscles. As the hips tip forward, the curve in the lower back increases. If you tuck your tail under, the curve of the lower back flattens.

1. Whilst standing side on to a mirror, try tucking and tilting the pelvis forwards and backwards. You may find this easier if you bend the knees slightly. Watch closely and see how much movement you have in each direction. Feel the muscles that are being used to move to each position. Find a position somewhere in the middle where the front of your pelvis is straight up and down. Make sure you are still relaxed and feel lengthened in your upper body.

2. Some people stand with an over increased curve, especially in their lower back, which means that they will have to focus on flattening the curves slightly.

3. Many dancers are taught to flatten out the curve in their low back. They do this by using their bottom muscles too much or bracing strongly with the abdominals. Unfortunately, this can make your back a little unstable.

4. Try finding "Neutral Spine" when you are on your hands and knees. Make sure that your knees are under your hips and your hands are under your shoulders.

5. Try finding the same position lying on your back. There should be a tiny space between the lowest part of your low back and the floor.

Part 1

The Tests and the Exercises

Stage 1

Fabulous Flexibility!

Why are Some People Flexible and Some Not?

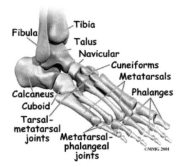

There are lots of little bones in your feet that let you walk over different surfaces, jump and point your toes. All of the bones in your body are joined together by little bands called ligaments. Some people have more stretch in their ligaments than others and so it is easier for them to turn out their hips and point their toes.

If a dancers' ligaments are very stiff, and hold the bones together tightly, they are called hypo-mobile. It can make it a little harder to point the feet, but the body is often more stable. Having a hypo-mobile foot can be a little annoying as the teacher may constantly be at you to "point your toes!", even when you are trying really hard. Luckily, we have written down some safe exercises and stretches that can help make your foot more flexible. Some people may teach unsafe stretches that you shouldn't do, so please only do very gentle stretches for your feet.

Other people have very stretchy ligaments in their feet and can point their feet easily. This is called a hyper-mobile foot. This may seem fantastic to the people with stiff feet, but it is sometimes harder to keep your arches up. If the ligaments are too stretchy, it means you have to have very strong muscles to control the feet. There are lots of good exercises in this book to train these muscles and make the most of having a hyper-mobile foot.

So How Much Flexibility Do You Need?

Stage 1 Tests

This stage is all about the flexibility in your ankles and feet. The more mobile they are, the easier it is to get right up onto your pointe shoes! Some people will find these tests easy than others and some may take a little longer to get there.

There are three tests that we need to do to check out the flexibility of your feet.
1) Demi-Pointe Range
2) Pointe Range
3) Toe To Wall Test (for plié depth)

For each test there is a check-list of things to watch for. On the pages after the tests there are some pictures and descriptions of some of the things you may be doing wrong. Remember that the pictures are exaggerations. The more subtle weaknesses are often very important, so be picky! If you can't check off each one of these points, mark a cross next to that point in The Workbook.

On Day 1, go through each of the exercises for that stage slowly with the instructions, and then complete them each day as written in the program.
Go back to the tests on Day 13 and see if you are ready to proceed to the next stage!

Test 1

Test	Weakness?	Day 1	Day 13
Demi-Pointe Range Test *(page 15)*	Reduced demi-pointe		
	Reduced pointe range		
	Toes clawing		
	Pain behind the ankle		
Pointe Range Test *(page 17)*	Reduced pointe range		
	Toes curling under		
	Ankles sickling in		
	Ankles sickling out		
	Knees bent		
	Pain behind the ankle		
Toe To Wall Test *(page 20)*	Heels lifting		
	Arches rolling		
	Less than 10cm		
	Pain at the front		

Test 1
Demi-pointe Range

It is very important that you can work your feet into a good height of demi-pointe. It helps in strengthening the ankles properly with rises, and allows you to work all the correct muscles in the feet in preparation for pointe work. If you find it hard to get onto demi-pointe, you will find it very hard to get onto full pointe and your ankles will be very wobbly!

1. Start in a sitting position on a chair or ball. Slowly, push the foot up into a demi-pointe position making sure to relax the toes. All the time keeping note that the rest of your body is relaxed but controlled.

2. If possible, push slightly over the demi-pointe to test your full range, but make sure to keep the ankle in line. Remember, you are only trying to test the range of the joints here and not the strength.

Checklist!
- Make sure that you achieve at least a 90° angle at your big toe joint.
- The front of the ankle should be flat or rounded forwards slightly
- Keep your toes long and relaxed on the floor.
- There should be no pain at the back of the ankle.

Common Problems with Demi-Pointe Test

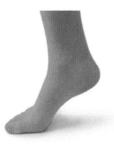

Reduced Demi-pointe Range

If your big toe is too stiff and does not allow you to go onto a full demi-pointe, usually the muscle that sits under the big toe is a bit tight. Massage it gently with a golf ball (or pinkie ball) or use your fingers to gently loosen the muscle. It is also good if you can warm up the muscles a little with a foot bath before you do this to get the blood flowing. Make when massaging your foot that your big toe is pulled back and as relaxed as possible. DO NOT push into this stretch if there is pain on the top of the big toe.

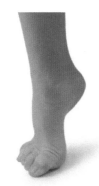

Toes Clawing

This will happen if you are very tight in the muscles on the sole of the foot or weak in the back of the calf. Doing the 'Calf Stretches' and the 'Foot Massage', after a warm foot bath, should help loosen them. Make sure that you always focus on keeping your toes long when you point your feet, and when you do rises.

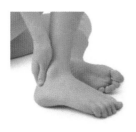

Pain at the Back of the Ankle

You should not experience pain with any of these tests or exercises. If there is still pain after stretching the calves and massaging the feet, check with your dance teacher if there is a local dance physiotherapist (physical therapist) that you can see. Do not push into the pain at the back of the ankle.

Reduced Pointe Range

It is very important to have a good range of pointe at the front of the ankle and the middle of the foot before you start pointe work. If the ankles are stiff you will need to bend the knee to be able to fully rise onto the platform of the shoe. PLEASE DO NOT stretch your feet forcefully using pianos, doors or any other technique you may see others do. Forced stretching may cause damage to the ligaments and prevent you from going onto pointe for a long time. Gentle stretching with the 'Pointe Stretch' will slowly stretch out the front of the foot, allowing you to pointe further.

Test 2
Pointe Range Test

It is also obviously very important to have good flexibility in the front of your ankles before starting en pointe. If you do not have enough range you will find that you have to bend the knees in order to get fully up onto your box en pointe. Often students with restricted range get irritation at the back of the ankle from trying so hard to rise.

1. Sit on the floor with your legs stretched out in front of you. Make sure that you are sitting up from your low back and not slumping! Keep your shoulders and neck relaxed. Sit on a towel or pillow if needed to keep your back straight.

2. Keeping your knees pulled up slowly point your toes and ankles as far as you can. Get your friend to measure your range using a 'Goniometer' or large protractor, or take a digital photo from the side and measure the angle from the lumpy bone on the outside of the shin (below your knee) through your ankle bone and to the middle of your little toe.

Checklist!

- Make sure that your toes are not curled under, but are pointed at the knuckle and stay almost straight in the middle joints. This takes practice!
- The ankles must be straight, not sickling in or out.
- Looking from the side, you should be able to draw a straight line from the lumpy bone on the outside of your knee, through your ankle joint and to your little toe joint.
- Keep your knee-caps pulled up.
- There should be no pain in the back of the ankle.

Common Problems with Pointe Range Test

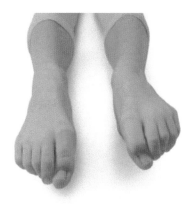

Clawing the Toes

If the toes are curling under or "clawing" when pointing your foot it usually means that the muscles deep in your calf are working too strongly and the small muscles in your feet are not strong enough. This is very important to master before going onto pointe as clawing of the toes in pointe shoes will lead to a line of blisters across your toe knuckles that can be very painful! The more control you can achieve in your small foot muscles, by doing exercises like 'Toe Swapping' and 'Pointe Through Demi-Pointe' later in this program, the easier it will be to pointe the foot properly. If you are using the deep calf muscles too much to point the foot, you can also develop overuse injuries very quickly when en pointe.

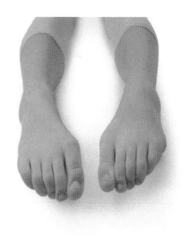

Sickling the Ankles In

Sickling in happens if you are weak along the outside of the ankle. Practice the 'Pointe through Demi-Pointe' exercise and really focus on keeping the ankle in line. Think of a straight line from the center of your knee, through the middle of your ankle and to your second toe. Also make sure that when you are rising or doing a relevé in class, you have your weight between your first and second toes, not rolling out onto the little toes.

Reduced Pointe Range

Sometimes you can have a good pointe range when you test for demi-pointe, but when you try to point the feet off the floor, they will not go as far. This means that you are not strong enough to make the most of your pointe range. Doing the 'Pointe through Demi-Pointe' and 'Seated Rises' will help you find all the different muscles to use when pointing the feet. Make sure you focus on using all of these muscles when you are doing a battement tendu in class.

"Fishing" Or Sickling Out

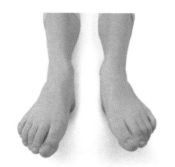

Some teachers and choreographers like the look of a slightly "fished" foot en l'air, as it can give a nice line, however you must not do it on your supporting foot. If you do this it will put strain on the ligaments in your arch and on the inside of your knee. Some girls fish the foot to make it look like they have more pointe range, especially if they are stiff down the outside of the foot. By completing the 'Golf Ball Massage' to loosen the muscles down the outside of the foot, this can then allow you to point the foot more easily. Often, fishing the foot is just a habit, so practice exercises like 'Pointe through Demi-Pointe' and 'Seated Rises', focusing on keeping the ankle aligned straight.

Bent Knees

Having tension in the top of the calf may stop you from extending the knee fully, so make sure you practice lots of the 'Calf Stretches' to open out the back of the knee. The knees will often bend if you are a little stiff in the front of the ankle and are trying to get more of a pointe. Working on your 'Pointe Stretch' may help with this. Make sure you focus on pulling up the knees with the inner part of the quads *(VMO)*.

Pain At The Back Of the Ankle

You should be getting pain with any of these tests or exercises. Try the 'Calf Stretches' and the 'Foot Massage'. If you are still experiencing pain, check with your dance teacher about a dance physiotherapist (physical therapist) that you can see. Do not push into the pain at the back of the ankle. You may have something known as posterior impingement that can worsen if you keep dancing on it. Work at controlling your arches, as pain at the back of the ankle can develop when the feet are continuously rolling in.

Test 3
Toe to Wall Test

This test helps you work out how much plié range you have. It also helps you work out where you are tight, and gives you an easy way to measure your progress!

1. To start, place a piece of tape on the floor, pointing out from the wall. Measure out 2cm intervals and make marks on the tape that you can see whilst standing. (Make sure you don't draw on the floor!) Alternatively, place a ruler on the floor so you can see the markings. Once set, stand facing the wall with your feet in parallel. Place one foot so that your big toe is against the wall, and bend your knee so that it touches the wall. This counts as zero.

2. Slowly, move your foot back along the tape, keeping your knee on the wall, until your heel begins to lift. Find the point where your foot is the furthest it can be away from the wall, whilst your heel is still on the floor. Make sure your foot remains in parallel and your knee is still touching the wall. Take recordings of exactly how far (in centimeters) you have been able to go. Then repeat the whole process on the other side.

Checklist!

- Keep your heel down! No cheating!
- Keep your foot in parallel, perpendicular to the wall.
- Keep your arches gently lifted. By rolling in you may get a little further but this is a false measure.
- It does not matter what the other foot is doing.
- The plié depth you need does depend on your height, but aim for at least 10cm on both sides. If you are very small (under 140cm tall) 8cm is sufficient, and if you are over 160cm tall, aim for 12cm.
- The range should be similar on each side.
- There should be no pain at the front of the ankle. You may feel a stretch along the tendons at the back of the ankle.

Common Problems with the Toe to Wall Test

Heels Coming Off the Floor
This happens if you are tight in the calves, or stiff in the front of the ankle joint. Do lots of work on your 'Calf Stretches'. Make sure you ground your heels properly when jumping, and work on all the exercises for the small muscles of your feet to take some of the pressure off your calves.

Arches Rolling In
This often happens if you are a little stiff at the back of the calf and are trying to achieve more range. It is also the case if your feet are very mobile and the arch muscles are not doing their job correctly! It's very important to hold the arches up gently to find your correct range. If you roll the feet in when in plié or en fondu you have more chance of getting knee problems and will have trouble keeping your balance on one leg. Focus on the 'Tripod Foot' and make sure you control the arches in class.

One Foot Measuring More Than the Other
This obviously shows that you are tighter in one ankle and calf than the other. Complete twice as many 'Calf Stretches' on your stiff side each day. Make sure you ground your heels properly when jumping, and work on all the exercises for the small muscles of your feet to take some of the pressure off your calves. Ask a parent or friend to massage your calves after dancing as this will also help. (Hint – trade Dad for a neck massage!)

Pain at the Front of the Ankle
You should not be experiencing pain with any of these exercises. Try the 'Pointe Stretch' and the 'Golf Ball Massage' after a warm foot bath. If the pain does not subside, check with your dance teacher about a dance physiotherapist (physical therapist) that you could see. Do not push into the pain at the front of the ankle.

Stage 1 Exercises

The Tripod Foot

1.   Stand with your feet flat on the floor in parallel. Roll your heel bones in and out before centering the weight in the middle of the heel. Slowly move your weight forwards and backwards. Feel where the points of pressure are under the foot and how they change as you move. Find a position where you can feel equal weight under the big and little toe joints, and slightly more pressure on the ball of the foot than the heel. Complete ten, 10 second holds every day.

Checklist!

- Make sure the legs are aligned with the knee caps facing forwards. If the knees are facing in, the lower legs will turn in and make the arches drop a little.

- Focus on turning the thighs out from your hips and watch what happens to your feet.

- Make sure that the arches are gently lifted, without rolling your weight too far onto the outer part of the foot.

- Relax the tendons at the front of the ankle, and hold this position for 10 seconds.

- Try closing your eyes and see how much more you are aware of and what exactly is going on in the feet!

Calf Stretches

Your calves can get very tight, especially if you are doing a lot of dancing. Make sure to do the bent knee stretch, as well as the more common straight leg stretch as this gets into the deeper muscles of the calf. These muscles often get tight if you have been doing lots of jumping or if you have been doing lots of rises in preparation for pointe work! These muscles can also work too hard to support hyper-mobile feet if the small foot muscles are not doing their job correctly.

1. Gastrocnemius - Keep your body upright. Have one foot forward and one foot back. Keep both heels on the floor, feet pointing straight ahead. Slowly bend the front knee, keeping the back knee straight, until a stretch is felt in the top of the calf of the back leg. Do three, 30 second holds on each leg.

2. Soleus - Start in the same position as for Gastrocnemius but have your feet closer together. Keep both heels on the floor, with your toes pointing straight ahead of you. Bend both knees, until you feel a stretch lower in the calf of the back leg. Do three, 30 second holds on each leg, and a 10 second hold after practicing any rises.

Checklist!
- Make sure that both feet are facing forward in parallel
- You should not feel any pinching or pain at the front of the ankle. If you do, focus on relaxing the tendons at the front when you are in first position, and perform frequent massage to the front of the shins and under the foot
- Keep your body upright and your tummy muscles on

Pointe Stretch

Having a good pointe range is essential before going up onto pointe. If you do not have enough range in the front of your ankle, you will have to bend the knee to get fully up onto the pointe platform. Otherwise you will be dancing on the back edge of the platform which is not very safe!

1. Kneel on the floor, with your legs in parallel. Make sure that your ankles are straight. The heels will be pressing up into your bottom. If there is a strong stretch across the front of your ankle, use a rolled up towel to reduce the stretch initially.

2. If there is a gentle stretch, hold this position and focus on relaxing the ankles while breathing normally. Make sure you just feel a gentle stretch across the front of the ankle and no pain in the back of the ankle.

3. If you do not feel a stretch, reach your hand around one knee and pull it gently up towards you. You should feel a gentle stretch across the front of the ankle. Hold for 10 seconds, breathing normally, and then repeat on the other side. Do this three times on each side.

Checklist!
- The big toes should not come together and touch.
- Make sure that you do not hitch the hip of the lifted leg, and your body should remain straight and elongated.
- If you feel that you are progressing well with this exercise after the first week, you can progress on to hold for 30 seconds on each side.

Foot Massage

The small foot muscles located on the top of and under the ball of the foot can be very tight in some people. If you notice that your toes tend to sit in a bent position even when relaxed this is a good thing to practice. It is also helpful if you find it very hard to pointe your toes from the knuckles. If the muscles on the top of the foot are too tight, it will be very hard to point the foot correctly.

1. Massage up the front of the shin in big long strokes. If this muscle is tight it will block your pointe range. The muscles may be tender but there should not be real pain with the massage.

2. Feel for the space between your big toe bone and your 2nd toe bone (1st & 2nd Metatarsals). Slowly work your way up from the web space between the toes up into the middle of the foot.

3. Do the same under the ball of the foot (try pulling your toes back to give a bit of a stretch). You will often feel some sharp points of tension. Work on these gently over time and you will see good results.

4. Try massaging up the inside of the calf muscle. This is especially good to work on if your toes scrunch up or if you have any pain at the back of the ankle. Test out your pointe range after massaging all area and see if you can feel the difference. Try trading your Mum or Dad for a foot massage on a regular basis!

Checklist!
- Try and imagine that you are massaging 1cm deep into your foot, rather than just on the skin.
- While you may feel quite tight and tender when you first start this massage, you should not feel pain afterwards.
- Focus on internally asking the muscles to relax rather than just forcing your way through!

Toe Swapping

This is one way to train the small muscles that help to control the toes when dancing, and is really helpful when progressing onto pointe. This will take time to perfect! While it may feel impossible at first, the control of these muscles will improve with regular practice. It is simply a matter of learning how to tell the nerves that control these muscles what to do!

1. Sit on a chair, with feet in parallel, and place your feet flat on the ground in the 'Tripod Foot' position. Make sure the inner arch and under surface of your foot is active. Slowly lift your big toes off the floor at the same time, keeping all your other toes down.

2. Then, practice the opposite, by leaving your big toes on the floor and raise all your small toes off the ground. Continue swapping between the big and little toes at least 20 times. Make sure that the arches of your feet stay on the floor, and that the foot does not twist or roll from side to side. The ball of the foot must stay in contact with the floor at all times. If you find this difficult to begin with, use your fingers to help isolate the movements initially.

3. Cramping simply indicates that the muscles are a little weak for what they are being asked to do! If you experience any cramping, stop the exercise and wiggle the foot around or massage it to increase the blood flow. Once the ramp has settled, try again.

Checklist!
- If the feet continue to cramp, try this exercise after you are warmed up.
- Make sure that the arches do not roll in, especially as you press your big toe down on the floor.
- Try one foot at a time or both together.
- Use your fingers as much as you need to get the toes isolating in the beginning.

Doming

This exercise takes time to master, but is essential to be able to point your toes correctly and keep them long in your pointe shoes, preventing a lot of blisters! If you find it difficult at first do not worry! Try massaging the foot again, especially on the top and bottom of the foot, and try it with your hands as well as your toes.

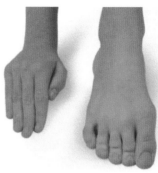

1. Sit on the floor with one foot forward and in parallel, keeping your toes long and relaxed. Keep your back lengthened and your knee in line with your ankle and 2nd toe.

2. Slowly press the under surface of the toes down and lift the ball of the foot away from the floor, as if you were trying to suck up the floor into your foot and leg. Be careful to keep your toes long and elongated. This will then create a dome under the knuckles. You can use your hands to mimic the movement if it makes it easier initially.

3. Maintain a gentle pressure through the tips of the toes and the centre of the heel. Keep toes long as they may curl under when you start this, but persevere! If the toes keep curling under, try bringing your heel back so that you are almost in a plié position. This can help switch off the extrinsic foot muscles that will work to claw the toes. When you have mastered this exercise sitting down, try practicing it standing up.

Checklist!
- Keep your toes long and straight in the middle knuckle!
- If you are very tight across the top of the foot, you may need to massage out the tension here before you strengthen too much.
- Use your hands to help your toes know where to go.
- Do not give up! This one may take practice but it is very important!

Pointe Through the Demi-Pointe

This exercise helps you understand how to work the little muscles that control your toes in isolation from the bigger muscles that pointe your ankle. This is very important in preventing overuse injuries in your legs, such as shin splints and stress fractures, as well as avoiding blisters on your toe knuckles in your pointe shoes!

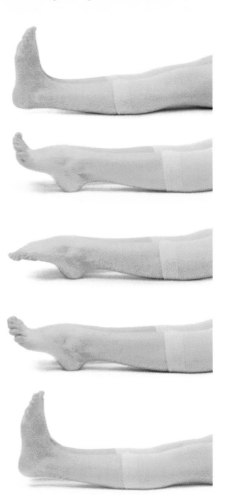

1. Sit on the floor, with your back straight and stomach held in, with the heels flexed

2. Slowly point the ankle, but not your toes i.e. demi-pointe in mid air. Remember to keep your knees pulled up and your toes elongated.

3. Slowly point your toes keeping them long. Make sure that you can see the knuckles where the toes join the foot, and that the toes are not curled under or clawing.

4. Now carefully flex your toes making sure to keep your ankle in the pointed position and your knees pulled up.

5. Flex your heel to complete this exercise and repeat the whole process 20 times. Draw circles with the ankle in between repetitions to keep the blood flowing and to stop any cramping in your calves or foot.

Checklist!
- Keep sitting up nice and straight.
- Keep the ankles aligned – no sickling or fishing!
- Keep your toes long in the middle knuckle; just point them from where they join onto your foot.
- You should feel the muscles under the ball of the foot begin to work.

Seated Rises

Use this exercise to learn how to train the small muscles of the foot and practice correct placement of the foot during a rise. Being able to do perfect rises is one of the best insurance policies against injuries! If you work the small muscles of the foot correctly, this takes the pressure off the deep calf muscles and the muscles in your shin.

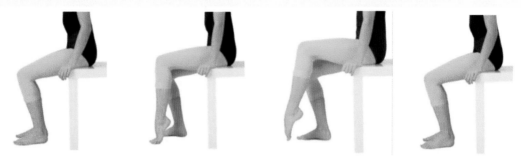

1. Sit on a chair, with the working foot flat on the floor. Make sure the inner arch and under surface of your foot is active.

2. Slowly begin to peel the foot off the floor, working the muscles of the foot. Make sure your ankle is in a straight line from the beginning. Push the foot slowly onto full demi-pointe and feel a stretch along the front of your ankle, and under your big toe. Make sure your foot is centered with your weight through the first and second toes, not "fishing" or "sickling" in any direction.

3. Lift the foot just off the floor, as though you were jumping and pointe the toes long in the air. Keep both sitting bones even on the chair and your back straight.

4. Slowly return the heel to the floor using gentle resistance to work the foot and keep your arch muscles engaged. Be sure that your toes are long and relaxed whilst keeping your arches active. Repeat slowly 20 times on each foot, concentrating on working all the muscles in your foot. You should not feel any pain in the foot at any stage.

Checklist!
- Keep your arches lifted as you lower the heel.
- Focus on peeling the foot up and down – as though it has 20 joints in it!
- Keep your knee aligned over your foot – try not to let it drop out to the side.

Big Toe Exercise

This is a great way to learn how to use the small muscle that sits under the big toe. It is important that this muscle is strong to support the front of the arch, to push off in jumps, and to rise smoothly from demi-pointe onto full pointe.

 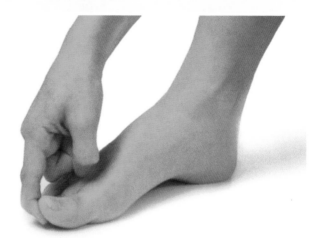

1. Kneel on one knee, with the other foot placed flat on the floor in front of you. Make sure that the weight is distributed evenly throughout the foot, with equal weight under your big and little toe joints. The inner arch and under surface of your foot should be active. Lift the big toe off the floor with your fingers making sure to keep the ball of the foot down.

2. Try and push your big toe down towards the floor using the muscle under the big toe, against the resistance of your fingers, and hold for 3 seconds. Make sure that the arches of the feet stay active and your foot should not twist in any direction. Slowly relax the contraction, and pull the toe back up. Repeat at least 20 times. The ball of the foot must stay in contact with the floor at all times. Be careful not to rock the weight onto the outside of the foot.

Checklist!
- Feel underneath the front of the foot to make sure that the big toe muscle is working.
- When it gets strong, you will be able to see it bulge a little when you contract it.
- Once you have mastered this exercise, try finding this muscle in standing by pressing the pad of the big toe down into the floor and lifting the big toe knuckle slightly.

Stage 1 Program

Day 1 is for testing and going through all the exercises slowly and to make sure that you are thinking of all the right things.

On Days 2 – 6 you can do the exercises every day.

Exercise	How many?	Day 2	Day 3	Day 4	Day 5	Day 6
The Tripod Foot	10 x 10 secs					
Calf Stretches	2 x 30 secs					
Pointe Stretch	3 x 10 secs					
Foot Massage	2 minutes					
Toe Swapping	20 reps					
Doming	20 reps					
Pointe Through Demi-Pointe	20 reps					
Seated Rises	20 reps					
Big Toe Exercise	20 reps					

Day 7 is a rest day!

On Days 8 – 12 you do the same exercises, but just a little more in each sitting.

Exercise	How many?	Day 8	Day 9	Day 10	Day 11	Day 12
The Tripod Foot	10 x 10 secs					
Calf Stretches	2 x 30 secs					
Pointe Stretch	3 x 30 secs					
Foot Massage	3 minutes					
Toe Swapping	2 x 20 reps					
Doming	2 x 20 reps					
Pointe Through Demi-Pointe	2 x 20 reps					
Seated Rises	2 x 20 reps					
Big Toe Exercise	2 x 20 reps					

Day 13 is when to retest yourself! See if you have improved enough to go onto the next stage. If the answer is yes, "Congratulations!" If not, don't worry; just repeat the second week of exercises again until you can do all three tests really well.

Stage 2

Marvelous Muscles!

The Foot Muscles

There are many tiny muscles in your feet that help control the bones. They start and end within the foot and are called your Intrinsic Foot Muscles.

Most people never even think of these muscles, let alone train them, but they are very important, especially in dancing. These muscles help you keep your balance, by making little changes when your walk over different surfaces. They are also very important when pointing your toes and balancing on demi-pointe.

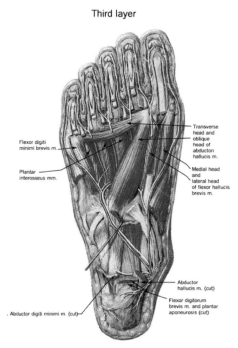

Third layer

Because we need to do special exercises to make these muscles strong, it is very common for them to be a little weak when you are first tested for pointe work. If we walked around outside without shoes on all day, climbing trees and walking in the sand, these muscles would naturally work and get very strong. However, most of us live in cities, and wear shoes most of the time, so our foot muscles get a little weak.

This does not mean that if you suddenly walk around in bare feet that your feet will get strong. If they are already weak it will take some time to build up enough strength to walk without support safely. Some people need to have special supports made to put in their shoes to hold their feet in the right place until they learn how to strengthen the muscles enough to do it themselves.

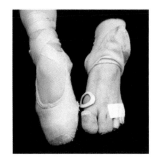

It is very important to get the intrinsic muscles strong before starting pointe work, because if you "claw" the toes in pointe shoes, you may get blisters on your toe knuckles that can be very painful! Also, if you look at the sole of most pointe shoes they are a little rounded. This makes it much harder to balance compared to standing in bare feet or regular ballet shoes.

Some people think that getting blisters and pain in the feet is just a part of pointe work, but this does not have to be the case! With strong feet and shoes that fit well from when you first start pointe, many girls have no pain at all!

The other muscles that help control your feet and ankles are called your Extrinsic Foot Muscles. They start in the lower leg, and then turn into little ropes called tendons that attach down into the feet and toes.

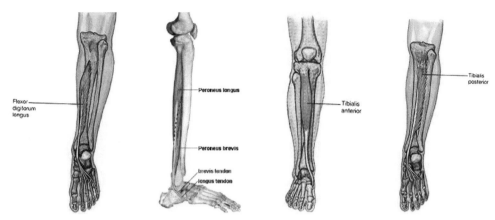

If

these muscles are too tight it may be hard to bend your knees or keep your heels down in a demi-plié. If these muscles are working more than your intrinsic foot muscles, your toes will "claw" under when you pointe your feet, or when you rise onto demi-pointe.

When they are over used these muscles can have problems such as tendonitis, or they may even cause a stress fracture in your shin bone. Many dancers feel clicking or grinding in the ankle when they perform rises, and this is usually a sign of irritation in these tendons.

Most of the stability in your feet comes from mastering control of the small muscles inside them. The more control you have in your intrinsic foot muscles and the muscles around your ankle, the more stable you will be in pointe shoes and the faster you will progress!

Chances are that one side will be much easier than the other, and it may be a little tricky when you first start. However, stick at it because if you focus lots of attention on your toes, it is amazing the control you can achieve.

Stage 2 Tests

Stage 2 is about building strength in your feet and ankles so that you can cope with the constant demands of pointe work. The more you can focus on isolating all the little muscles in your feet the better! The more control you have of your intrinsic foot muscles before you start pointe work, the easier it is!

On Day 1 do the two tests and mark down which parts you have trouble with then, go over the exercises for that section. Follow the program on the next page for at least two weeks before retesting.

Test	Weakness	Day 1	Day 13
Single Leg Standing *(page 36)*	Clawing toes		
	Ankle rocking		
	Arches rolling		
	Big toe joint lifting		
	Gripping tendons		
	Hip hitching		
	Hip dropping		
Single Leg Rises *(page 40)*	Leaning forward		
	Clawing toes		
	Reduced demi-pointe height		
	Sickling out		
	Sickling in		
	Bending the knees		
	Losing turnout		
	Rolling arches		
	Unable to do 15 rises		
	Pain behind the ankle		

Remember to make sure you can perform the tests really well before moving onto the next stage. It doesn't matter if you spend three or four weeks on each stage as it will make the next stage a much easier process to go through.

Test 4
Single Leg Standing - Parallel and Turnout

This sounds so simple, but many dancers find it really hard! Being able to balance on one leg is very important before progressing onto pointe. The bottom of a pointe shoe is a little bit unstable, so if you are wobbling when standing on one leg in bare feet, you will be very unstable in pointe shoes.

1. Start by standing on one leg in parallel remembering to pointe the toe of the lifted foot. Keep your hands placed on your hips and look straight ahead focusing on a point on the wall. Make sure not to look at your feet!

1. Hold this position for at least 10 seconds and then repeat on the other side. Feel that you have a little more weight over the ball of your foot than on the heel.

2. Repeat the process in turnout again with your hands in bra bas. Make sure you keep your hips facing forward whilst keeping your feet turned out. Hold this position for at least 10 seconds.

Checklist!
- Keep your toes long and relaxed, not gripping the floor.
- 3. Make sure the foot is stable, not rocking from side to side.
- The arches should stay gently lifted.
- Make sure the big toe joint and little toe joint are both on the floor.
- The tendons at the front of the ankle are reasonably relaxed. Occasional flickers are okay, constant gripping and clawing is not!

Common Problems with Single Leg Standing

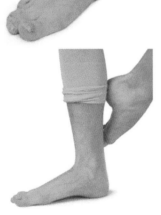

Toes Gripping
If the toes are gripping the floor it usually means that the extrinsic muscles are pulling too strongly and the intrinsic muscles of the toes are not strong enough. Strengthening these small muscles with the toe exercises, and working on the stability of your ankles with the 'Balance Exercises' will help enormously.

Arches Dropping/Rolling In
Many girls blame the shape of their foot for the amount that they roll, and while there are many different shaped feet around, most often it is the muscles that are weak! Your inside arch muscles and the muscle that sits under the big toe are very important. Really focus on feeling these muscles work with all the exercises, and the control of your feet will improve in no time! Also, make sure that you are turning the leg out from the hips. If the hip turns in, the knee turns in and then the foot rolls in!

Rolling Out
Make sure that while you are concentrating on not rolling in, you don't over compensate and start rolling out! Your weight should be spread 60% on the ball of the foot, 40% on the heel, and evenly distributed between the big and little toe joints. Remember the 'Tripod Foot' from Stage 1.

Tendon Gripping
If the tendons are gripping at the front of the ankle it usually means that you are holding too much weight back on the heel. Try shifting your weight so that 60% of your weight is on the ball of the foot. If the tendons are still flicking on and off or gripping strongly, the intrinsic muscles of the foot and arch probably still need strengthening, so focus on all the little foot exercises.

Losing Turnout in the Hips

True turnout is controlled by the muscles deep in the back of the hip. We will work on turnout more in the next stage, but try to stay turned out from behind the hip, rather than from the feet or the knees, whenever you are standing in turnout. The 'Turnout Exercise in Retiré' will help you learn where to focus your attention.

Dropping the Hip

Dropping the hip of the lifted leg usually means that the muscles in your centre and down the outside of the supporting hip are not strong enough and cannot do their job! For now, just focus on keeping your hips level and holding your turnout from behind the hip. Doing the 'Side Lifts' will help strengthen your midsection muscles so you can control this better.

Hitching the Hip

Hitching the hip is another common compensation if you are weak in the hips or middle section. Make sure your hips are level, and keep your tummy muscles engaged! Keep the foot a little lower when practicing retiré until you get an idea of how to hold the hips still.

The Calf Muscles

When you start pointe work, you will not be doing pirouettes, fouettés or penchés straight away. You will do rises, rises, maybe some relevés and then more rises! It is important that you know all the correct things to think about and practice perfect rises on demi-pointe first, as this will make beginning pointe work much easier.

You have two main calf muscles - Gastrocnemius and Soleus that both attach into your Achilles (or calcaneal) tendon and then feed down into your heel bone (calcaneus).

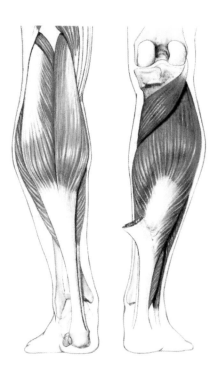

As the long calf muscles (Gastrocnemius) attach just above the knee joint, they can bend the knee as well as pointe the ankle. Make sure you keep the knees pulled up when doing your rises.

If your calf muscles are nice and strong, they will also take the load off the smaller Extrinsic Foot Muscles that were mentioned earlier, resulting in fewer ankle injuries!

Test 5
Single Leg Rises in Parallel

1. Stand on one leg in the parallel resting your finger tips gently on a wall or barre. Hold the lifted leg in just off the floor with the foot pointed. Make sure that the arches of the supporting foot are lifted.

2. Slowly rise up onto a full demi-pointe and then lower slowly. Repeat this exercise and many times as you can (up to 20 times).

Checklist!

- Keep your chest lifted, with your spine in neutral and abdominal muscles on.
- Keep the lifted foot pointed at the ankle, with the thigh turned out from the hip.
- Toes remain long – no clawing!
- Rise to the full height of demi-pointe.
- Keep your weight centered between the first and second toes.
- The knee on your supporting leg remains pulled up throughout.
- The little toe on the other leg should still stay in contact with the floor.
- Hips remain facing forward.
- Turnout of the foot is maintained as you lower the heel.
- Arches stay lifted at all times.
- At least 15 perfect rises.
- There should be no pain in the back of the ankle or big toe.
- The body must stay upright, not leaning forwards or backwards, or to either side.

Common Problems with Single Leg Rises

Body Leaning Forward

In most cases, if the body is tipping forward it means that you are weak in the calves, and are trying to use the body's momentum to get up onto demi-pointe. It will often happen more as the foot and ankle get tired. The solution to this is simply awareness and strength! Remember all the check-list points, and practice 'Single Leg Rises in Parallel' to increase your calf strength and foot control. This will then save you the worry of thinking about turnout at the same time! If the body tips off to the side, it usually means that the muscles down the outside of the supporting hip are not doing their job. Focus on keeping the hips square, and your tummy muscles on! The 'Turnout Exercise in Retiré' should help strengthen this area, and we will work more on the strength of the hips in Stage 3.

Clawing

If the toes are "clawing" when you perform a rise it may mean that the extrinsic muscles are working too strongly, the intrinsic muscles are tight and weak, and/or the calf muscles are not strong enough. Strengthen your calves by doing 'Double Leg Rises' in sets of 10, gradually building the amount you can do in one session, then progressing to single leg rises when you can maintain a good foot position.

Continue to work on the strength of the intrinsic foot muscles and massage any tight muscles in your feet with a 'Golf Ball' to make it easier to get onto demi-pointe. Doing the 'Soleus Stretch' may also help stretch the extrinsic foot muscles deep in the calf.

Losing Turnout

Even when you are working in parallel, it is important to use your turnout muscles to control the alignment of the hips. The turnout muscles are muscles deep in the back of the hip. Try 'Turnout Exercise in Retiré' to find the turnout muscles, and then repeat the rises, focusing on the same muscles. The 'Side Lifts' exercise will also help to strengthen the core muscles, which help in keeping the hips square.

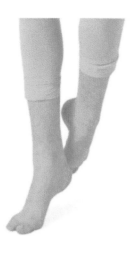

Reduced Height of Demi-Pointe

If you can demonstrate a good demi-pointe position when you are sitting, and not with rises, it means that you need more strengthening. If this is the problem, practice 'Double Leg Rises' in bigger sets (up to 30) and then try the single leg version. If it is not possible to achieve demi-pointe fully even when you are sitting, the big toe joint and the front of the ankle are probably too stiff. Go back to the Stage 1 exercises to loosen up the feet and improve your range. Also try using a warm foot bath for at least ten minutes before doing these exercises to help soften and warm up the muscles and ligaments.

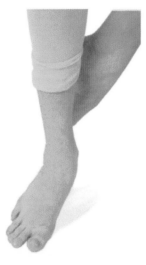

Sickling Out/Fishing

Sickling out or rolling onto the big toe happens if you are weak along the inside of the ankle. Some teachers and choreographers like the look of a slightly "fished" foot en l'air, however you must not do it on your supporting foot. Fishing can be very dangerous to the ligaments on the inside of the foot and ankle. Fishing en pointe may result in the shank (sole) of the shoe twisting away from under the sole of the foot. Focus on keeping the ankle in line with all of these exercises coming onto the demi-pointe.

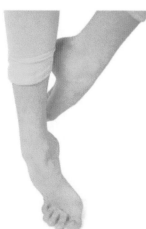

Sickling In

Sickling in happens when you are weak along the outside of the ankle. Complete 'Rises with Theraband' with the band on the inside of the ankle to find and strengthen the correct muscles.

Some people start sickling out because they are too tight in their big toe joint. Test your demi-pointe position again and if it is tight, do the 'Golf Ball Massage' to loosen the muscles under the big toe, and the 'Seated Rises' before working on your rises.

Bending the Knee

You may be tempted to bend the knee when rising if you have a restricted pointe range. Bending the knee allows you to get higher onto the demi-pointe, but is not very graceful! Keep practicing the Stage 1 exercises until you have a good pointe range. You may also bend the knees if you are not strong enough in the calves, or when your calves tire. Build up you endurance by doing sets of 'Double Leg Rises' and gradually build to doing single leg rises.

Rolling Arches on Lowering

To stop the arches rolling in as you lower the heel, do the 'Arch Awareness Exercise' and practice 'Seated Rises' to feel what muscles you have to use to control the arch. When you are doing rises, try and make it look like you don't really want to come down; that you are just grounding the heel, and are ready to go back up again. A dancer who drops her arches and thumps the heel down will not be particularly graceful en pointe!

Pain at the Back of the Ankle

You should not be feeling pain with any of these exercises. Try the 'Calf Stretches' and the 'Golf Ball Massage' If there is still pain, check with your dance teacher about a dance Physiotherapist (physical therapist) that you can see. Do not push into the pain at the back of the ankle. Work on controlling your arches, as pain can develop when the feet are rolling in frequently, or if you are not using your intrinsic foot muscles enough.

Unable To Perform Fifteen Repetitions

Sometimes a dancer can do lovely rises when she focuses but is just too weak to do fifteen of them. The solution to this is simply strength! Remember all the check-list points, and practice 'Single Leg Rises in Parallel' to increase your calf strength and foot control, without the worry of thinking about turnout at the same time! Build it up in sets of 5-10 rises. Good times to practice are when you are brushing your teeth in the morning and night, and when waiting for people! Make sure you do your 'Calf Stretches' after practicing the rises.

Stage 2 Exercises

Balance Exercises

Having good balance comes from a few different places. You have little cells on the surfaces of your joints and in the tendons and ligaments around the joints that tell your brain where your joints are in space. This is called 'proprioception'. If you have sprained your ankle or knee in the past, these cells may not be working very well and your ankle may wiggle from side-to-side when you stand on one leg or on demi-pointe.

1. Try balancing on one foot in parallel or in turnout. Focus on the position of your foot (tripod foot position) and relaxing your upper body. Make sure that your hips stay level and your arches are on.

2. Balance is also helped by your vision, which is why it is so important to "spot" when you are doing pirouettes. Try balancing on one leg with your eyes shut and see how much harder it is! It is good to practice like this as it challenges the other feedback systems more.

3. The third thing that helps with your balance is a system of loops filled with fluid deep inside your ear. When you move your head or body, the fluid should stay level and will tell your brain where you are in space. But if there is sudden movement, the movement of the fluid can be confusing. Try turning your head from side-to-side when doing the exercises to challenge this part of your balance.

4. You can also try standing on a wobble board. Do this on two legs first, and then on one. You can also combine any of the variations to challenge yourself even more!

Checklist!
- Try practicing tests like this in class.
- Try doing a few barre exercises each day with your eyes closed. This means that you have to really think about the choreography to!
- Practice while you are on the phone or when watching TV, or while waiting at the bus stop.
- Frequent little bits of balance training are better than one big session.

Toe Swapping

This is one way to train the small muscles that help to control the toes when dancing, and is really helpful when progressing onto pointe. This will take time to perfect! While it may feel impossible at first, the control of these muscles will improve with regular practice. It is simply a matter of learning how to tell the nerves that control these muscles what to do!

1. Sit on a chair, with feet in parallel, and place your feet flat on the ground in the 'Tripod Foot' position. Make sure the inner arch and under surface of your foot is active. Slowly lift your big toes off the floor at the same time, keeping all your other toes down. Make sure that the ball of the foot stays on the floor, and that your lower leg stays in the same place!

2. Then, practice the opposite, by leaving your big toes on the floor and raise all your small toes off the ground. Make sure that the foot does not twist or roll from side to side. The ball of the foot must stay in contact with the floor at all times. If you find this difficult to begin with, you can use your fingers to help isolate the movements.

3. Cramping simply indicates that the muscles are a little weak for what they are being asked to do! If you experience any cramping, stop the exercise and wiggle the foot around or massage it to increase the blood flow. Once the cramp has settled, try again.

Checklist!
- If the feet continue to cramp, try this exercise after you are warmed up.
- Make sure that the arches do not roll in, especially as you press your big toe down on the floor.
- Try one foot at a time or both together.
- Use your fingers as much as you need to get the toes isolating in the beginning.

Doming

This exercise takes time to master, but is essential to be able to pointe your toes correctly and to keep them long in your pointe shoes, preventing a lot of blisters! Once you have mastered it, try and think of this exercise while you are in class and whenever you are pointing your toes to wake up all of the muscles in the ball of your foot.

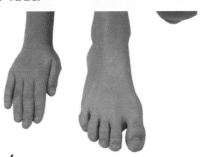 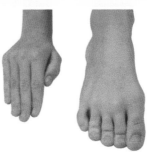

1. Sit with one foot in front of you in parallel with the toes long and relaxed. Make sure that the center of your heel is on the floor, and there is equal weight under the joint of your big toe and your little toe. Place your hand down next to your foot (doing it with your hand at the same time helps your brain work out how to tell your foot what to do!

2. Slowly lift the skin of the ball of the foot and the palm of the hand off the floor by pressing the undersurface of the toes and fingers into the floor and drawing the pads slightly in towards you. Be careful to keep your toes and fingers long. This will then create a dome under the knuckles. Maintain a gentle pressure through the tips of the toes and the centre of the heel. Your toes may curl under when you start this, but persevere!

3. When you have mastered this exercise sitting down, try integrating it into a tendu to second. Tendu to a demi pointe position, and then do the doming exercise to fully point the foot. This is also how you will be pointing your toe in your pointe shoes!

Checklist!
- If you are very tight across the top of the foot, you may need to massage out the tension here before you strengthen too much.
- Use your hands to help your toes know where to go.
- Do not give up! This one may take practice but it is very important!

Piano Playing

Now this one will definitely take time to perfect! Being able to do this exercise is not a definite requirement before going onto pointe, but it will help improve the control of your toes a lot. It is often very hard to separate the second and third toes when you start this exercise. Keep working at it and you will be surprised how much you will improve. The more practice you do, the better you will get with these exercises. You can do them in your shoes, at school, waiting for the bus and while watching TV. Test the rest of your family and see if any of them can do this exercise!

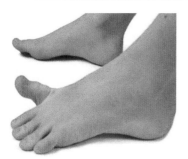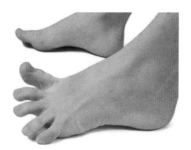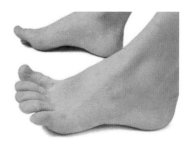

1. Set your feet up as for the toe swapping. Keep the ball of the foot flat on the floor throughout this exercise. Slowly lift the big toe off the floor keeping all of the other toes down.

2. One by one lift each of the other toes off the floor, keeping the ball of the foot flat on the floor. Make sure that the center of the heel is still engaged with the floor. Try not to roll the foot onto the outer edge.

3. Once all of the toes are lifted, start placing your toes back down on the floor starting with your little toe (pinkie) all the way through to your big toe. Make sure that the arches of your feet stay engaged and your foot does not roll in as you bring the big toe down to the floor.

Checklist!
- Use your hands to help your toes know where to go in the beginning.
- Using your hands alongside your feet can also help you make the right message in your brain to send to your feet.
- Do not give up! This one may take practice but it is very important!
- Make sure that the middle part of the foot does not roll in!

Pointe Through Demi-pointe

This exercise helps you understand how to work the little muscles that control your toes in isolation from the bigger muscles that pointe your ankle. This is very important in preventing overuse injuries in your legs, such as shin splints and stress fractures, as well as avoiding blisters on your toe knuckles in your pointe shoes!

1. Sit on the floor, with your back straight and stomach held in, with the heels flexed

2. Slowly point the ankle, but not your toes i.e. demi-pointe in mid air. Remember to keep your knees pulled up and your toes elongated.

3. Slowly point your toes keeping them long. Make sure that you can see the knuckles where the toes join the foot, and that the toes are not curled under or clawing.

4. Now carefully flex your toes making sure to keep your ankle in the pointed position and your knees pulled up.

5. Flex your heel to complete this exercise and repeat the whole process 20 times. Draw circles with the ankle in between repetitions to keep the blood flowing and to stop any cramping in your calves or foot.

Checklist!

- Make sure that your ankles are nicely aligned. There should be a straight line from the center of your knee, through the middle of your ankle and on to your second toe,
- There should not be any pain in the back of the ankle.
- Makes sure that your toes stay straight in the middle knuckle. If you find this difficult at first, do more of the doming exercise and foot massage.

Rises with Theraband

Using the Theraband is a very good way to strengthen the muscles that are on the outside of the ankle. It is important that these muscles are strong so they are able to control the ankle in demi or full pointe, especially if you tend to sickle out!

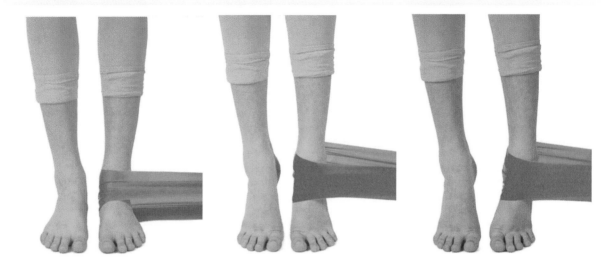

1. Place a resistance band around the inside of one ankle, and loop the other end around a table leg. Stretch out the band so that there is tension in it. Stand with your feet in the tripod foot position.

2. Slowly rise onto demi-pointe, keeping your weight centered and the ankle straight. Feel the muscles along the outside of the ankle working to keep it in line. Slowly lower the heels, keeping your arches on, and your toes lengthened. Practice at least 10 rises in this position, before placing the band around the other foot.

3. Make sure that your weight does not roll onto the outside of the foot causing you to sickle. Focus on keeping your weight centered between your big toe and your second toe.

Checklist!
- There should not be any pain under your big toe. If there is, place a soft towel under the ball of the foot, with your big toe off the edge.
- Makes sure that both feet are nicely aligned by doing this exercise in front of a mirror

Single Leg Rises in Parallel

Having good strength and form with single leg rises in parallel is essential in preventing most foot and ankle injuries. These exercises should be practised consistently. You may lightly rest your fingertips on the wall if you need help in maintaining your balance!

1. Stand on one foot in parallel with the other foot pointed at the side of your ankle. Remember to keep you supporting knee pulled. Have your arms relaxed by your side and keep your shoulders down.

2. Slowly rise up to your full height of demi pointe. Keep your weight centred between your first and second toe and your toes long. Repeat 15 times on each foot. Make sure to gently stretch your calves after doing this exercise.

Checklist!
- Make sure that your toes stay long throughout the exercise
- Keep your arches lifted as you lower the heels.
- Your toes should not lift of the ground.
- Make sure that you go directly up and down. Avoid rocking the body forward to help you rise.
- Keep your hips level and facing the front
- Make sure you try to reach to your full height of demi-pointe.
- Make sure you keep your knees pulled up.
- Keep your ankle aligned throughout – use a mirror to check initially

Turnout Exercise in Retiré Position

This is a fantastic way to find your turnout muscles and learn to use them without anything else around the hips. Make sure you keep your tummy muscles on, and that your back and hips stay still.

1. Lie on your stomach with your legs in parallel. Bend one knee to 90° and take it out to the side slightly. Loop a resistance band around your ankle, and have the other end around a table leg or a friend's knee. Keep your hips in line (no hitching) and both hip bones on the floor. Have one hand under your forehead and the other under you hip to check for lifting of the hip.

2. Slowly bring the lifted foot towards the leg on the ground, as though you are going into a retiré position. Pause, then slowly release, letting the leg come back to the starting position. Repeat ten times on one leg, keeping your hips still, then repeat on the other side. Complete two sets of ten on each leg.

Checklist!
- Make sure you are using your deep turnout muscles and not gripping with your outer bottom muscles.
- Remember to release SLOWLY, so that you are working the muscles on the way up as well as the way down.

Piriformis Stretch

The piriformis is one of your biggest turnout muscles. This is a wonderful stretch for releasing tension deep in the back of the hips, and is perfect after any exercise focusing on turning out. It can also help with improving your flexibility for the splits and into turnout.

1. Lie on your back, with one leg stretched out straight. Bend the other knee up halfway towards your chest. Use the same hand as the bent knee to push the leg halfway across your body. Use the other hand to gently pull the shin of the lifted leg towards you.

2. You should feel a deep stretch in the bottom of the lifted leg. You should NOT feel pinching in the front of the hip. If you are feeling pain rather than a releasing stretch take care not to pull your knee in too far to your chest. Hold for 30 seconds, repeating twice each side.

Checklist!
- Make sure both sides of the pelvis stay in contact with the ground.
- The spine stays in neutral with the tail-bone on the ground.
- There should not be any pinching or pain in the front of the hip. If there is, do the 'Hip Flexor Stretch' in Stage 4 instead.

Side Lifts

This is an excellent way to improve your core strength and is great if you tend to shift the ribs to one side when rising. One side is usually a lot harder than the other, so do twice as many sets of 10 on the weaker side.

1. Start by lying on your side with your head resting on your arm (like a pillow). Rest the fingertips of the other hand gently on the floor. Make sure your feet are a little bit further forward than your hips. Gently contract your deep back and tummy muscles. Your back should be kept straight so that your waist should not be touching the floor.

2. Slowly, lift both legs just off the floor until your big toes are as high as your tummy button. Relax your shoulders (especially the top one) and breathe normally. Hold the legs off the floor for 5 seconds and repeat for 10 repetitions each side. If this is too hard in the beginning, start by lifting the top leg only and practice stabilizing in this position. Once you feel strong enough then try both legs at once.

Checklist!
- Make sure your underneath side (i.e. waist) is still pulled up off the floor and not touching.
- Keep your neck long and relaxed
- Try not to press down too hard with your hand into the floor.
- If you can do this easily, try having your hand on your hip instead of on the floor.

Stage 2 Program

Day 1 is for testing and going through all the exercises slowly, to make sure that you are thinking of all the right things.

On Days 2 – 6 you can do the exercises every day.

Exercise	How Many?	Day 2	Day 3	Day 4	Day 5	Day 6
Balance Exercises	10 x 10 secs					
Toe Swapping	20 reps					
Doming	10 reps					
Piano Playing	10 reps					
Pointe through Demi Pointe	20 reps					
Rises With Theraband	2 x 10 reps					
Single Leg Rises in Parallel	15 reps/leg					
Turnout Exercise In Retiré	2 x 10 reps					
Piriformis Stretch	2 x 30 secs					
Side Lifts	2 x 10 reps					

Day 7 is a rest day!

On Days 8 – 12 you repeat the same exercises with just a little more in each sitting.

Exercise	How many?	Day 8	Day 9	Day 10	Day 11	Day 12
Balance Exercises	10 x 15 secs					
Toe Swapping	30 reps					
Doming	20 reps					
Piano Playing	20 reps					
Pointe through Demi Pointe	20 reps					
Rises With Theraband	2 x 10 reps					
Single Leg Rises in Parallel	20 reps/leg					
Turnout Exercise In Retiré	3 x 10 reps					
Piriformis Stretch	3 x 30 secs					
Side Lifts	3 x 10 reps					

Day 13 is when to retest yourself to see if you have improved enough to proceed to the next stage.

Stage 3

Terrific Turn out!

Your Turnout Muscles

As you can probably tell by some of the corrections on the 'Single Leg Standing Test' and with the 'Rises' tests, being strong enough to get onto pointe is not all about the feet. Having good turnout range and strength is very important before going onto pointe. Because the platform of a pointe shoe is so small, it is impossible to "cheat" turnout by screwing the feet around as some dancers try to do when on the flat!

While we are all constantly told to use our "turnout muscles", many of us don't actually know where they are. Looking at the pictures and working out just where these muscles are in your body can help so much in finding and working them. There are also some other very important muscles in the hips that we need for stability, there are pictures of these as well.

It is very important to control your turnout when en fondu (bending the knee). If you lose turnout from your hip en fondu, the knee rolls in and the foot rolls in. This not only looks bad, but puts the knee and ankle at risk of injury. During all of the tests and exercises in this section, focus on keeping turned out from the hip, not just the feet!

Gluteal Muscles

If you could take all the skin off your bottom, you would see many muscles underneath. First in line are your gluteals, or buttock muscles. Gluteus Maximus is the large one helping you to jump, control a fondu, and get your leg up in derrière. Gluteus medius sits more on the outside of your hip and helps you hold the hips level when standing on one leg, or when walking (models who swing their hips are not so good at using these!).

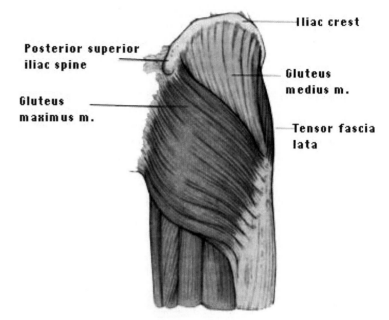

Posterior superior iliac spine

Gluteus maximus m.

Iliac crest

Gluteus medius m.

Tensor fascia lata

Turnout Muscles

Underneath the Gluteal Muscles are the muscles that control most of your turnout. You don't need to know all their names, but together they are known as the deep external rotators. It is important to use them for turning out so that you don't overuse the front of the hips (many dancers do this). Your inner thighs can help out a little with turnout as well, but in the turnout exercises, these deep muscles in the bottom are the ones you need to focus on.

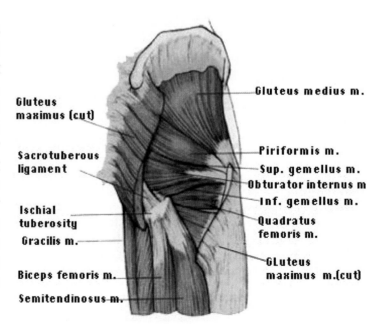

Gluteus maximus (cut)

Sacrotuberous ligament

Ischial tuberosity

Gracilis m.

Biceps femoris m.

Semitendinosus m.

Gluteus medius m.

Piriformis m.

Sup. gemellus m.

Obturator internus m

Inf. gemellus m.

Quadratus femoris m.

GLuteus maximus m.(cut)

Stage 3 Tests

Stage 3 is about controlling turnout from the hips and building stability in the hips to help you balance en pointe. Focus on finding the deep turnout muscles with each of the turnout exercises and then try and use them in class!

Test	Weakness	Day 1	Day 13
Plié In First Position	Heels lifting		
(page 58)	Arches rolling		
	Big toe lifting		
	Toes clawing		
	Knees coming forward		
	Chest tilting forward		
	Bottom sticking out		
	Bottom tucking under		
	Unable to keep balance		
	Pain at the front		
	Uneven bend in knees		
Single Knee Bends	Body leaning forward		
(page 61)	Body leaning back		
	Hip hitching		
	Hip dropping		
	Toes clawing		
	Bottom tucking under		
	Bottom sticking out		
	Knee dropping in		
	Losing turnout		

If you can learn to use the correct muscles for turnout in class, you will help prevent a lot of injuries and will achieve a greater strength more quickly. Do not worry about losing flexibility as you get stronger. Having strong stable hips will actually help make you more flexible and will make stretching much easier.

Test 6
Plié in First Position

A simple plié often tells so much about how a dancer can control her hips, feet and legs. Watch closely to pick up as many things as you can in order to make the best improvement.

1. Start by standing in first position with your hands on your hips. Take care with where you place your feet and keep pulled up through your knees. Make sure your deep core muscles are on, but keep your upper body relaxed.

2. Slowly bend your knees so as to achieve a demi-plié. Take note of any areas of tension or restriction. Now straighten the knees slowly coming back to a standing position. Repeat this exercise four more times.

Check List!

- Your heels must stay in contact with the floor at all times.
- Arches are to stay lifted.
- Both the big toe joint and little toe joint stay in contact with the floor.
- Toes are to remain long and relaxed.
- When bending your knees they are to stay out over your second toes.
- There should be the same amount of bend in each leg.
- Your chest and upper body should stay upright.
- Your bottom should not stick out or tuck under.
- You should be able to keep your balance for at least five pliés.
- There should be no pain at the front of the ankle or in the arch.
- Either side.

Common Problems with Plié in First Position

Forcing Turnout

Many dancers overturn their first position, and end up rolling the feet in. This is a fabulous way to give yourself an injury so is best avoided! Remember that most of your turnout should come from the hips, and only a little from the feet and ankles. The 'Parallel to Turnout' exercise in this section will help strengthen the turnout muscles.

Knees Rolling In

This can happen if you have overturned your feet, or if the turnout muscles are not controlling the hips as you bend. Try 'Turnout Exercise in Kneeling' to isolate your turnout muscles, and then the 'Functional Turnout Exercise' to strengthen the turnout muscles in a plié position.

Heels Coming Off the Floor

This usually happens if you are tight in the calves. Make sure you are doing your 'Calf Stretches' after practicing your rises, and you can also try stretching the calf by pressing the heel off the edge of a step during the day.

Bottom Sticking Out

This usually happens if you don't have very good turnout in the hips, and are tilting the hips forward to try to get more range. Work on your 'Inside Thigh Stretches' and the 'Piriformis Stretch Variations' to improve your range of turnout, and focus on the 'Functional Turnout Exercise' to strengthen the turnout muscles in a plié position. Make sure you are keeping your tummy muscles engaged!

Bottom Tucking Under

Many girls try too hard not to stick their bottom out and end up over compensating and tucking it under. You need to keep a "neutral spine" position, with just the smallest curve in your lower back, for the entire process of a plié. "Tucking" happens if you are trying to use your gluteals to turnout with instead of your turnout muscles. Practice a plié side on to a mirror to check your position.

Pain at the Front of the Ankle

You should not be getting pain with any of these exercises. Try the 'Pointe Stretch' and the 'Golf Ball Massage'. If you are still experiencing pain, check with your dance teacher about a dance physiotherapist (physical therapist) that you can see. Do not push into the pain at the front of the ankle.

One Knee Bending More Than the Other

This may happen if you are tighter in one ankle and calf than the other. Do the 'Toe To Wall Test' again, to see the difference, then work on your 'Calf Stretches', completing twice the amount on the stiffer side. Make sure you always ground your heels properly when jumping!

Test 7
Single Knee Bends - Parallel and Turnout

This test is a great way to assess how well your turnout muscles are controlling your hips and the general alignment of the leg. If your turnout muscles are a little weak then your knee and foot will tend to roll in. This is one of the biggest causes of knee problems, so if you have any knee pain take special note of this test!

1. Prepare to stand on one leg in parallel, with your hands placed on your hips. Your other foot should be pointed and kept away from your ankle.

2. Whilst keeping your spine lengthened, slowly bend the supporting knee to a deep fondu. Make sure to keep your heel down and arches activated. Slowly straighten the supporting leg, returning to a standing position. Repeat this exercise 5 times on both sides.

3. Repeat the exercise with turnout. Keep your hips facing forward and your knee over your second toe. Check in the mirror that you hips are level.

Checklist!
- Keep your body upright! Don't lean forward or back.
- Make sure that your knee stays in line with your second toe.
- Keep your hips level.
- Keep arches of the supporting foot on.
- No clawing of the toes.
- Make sure spine stays in neutral, no tucking!
- Watch the outside of your hip to make sure that it doesn't stick out.

Common Faults with Single Knee Bend

Body Leaning Forward

In most cases the common error with this exercise is tilting your upper body forward, once you have reached full fondu, if the bottom, back and abdominal muscles are not strong enough. Focus on strengthening your centre and engaging the muscles in your bottom by practicing the 'Three Legged Cat Exercise'. Make sure that when you practice the 'Single Knee Bends' you are thinking of using muscles deep in your bottom to help control you as you rise and lower. This also helps to avoid big bulky thighs!

Bottom Tucking Under

If the deep back muscles and bottom muscles are slightly weak, you may tend to tuck your tail under when bending rather than tilting your upper body forwards. When practicing the 'Three Legged Cat Exercise' or the 'Turnout Exercise in Kneeling', focus on keeping a small arch in the lower back as you move the leg. Practice the 'Single Knee Bends' side on to a mirror and watch your lower back closely to see if it moves.

Knee Coming In

The knee coming in is usually a sign that you are either not using the turnout muscles to control the position of your thigh, or your supporting foot is rolling in. Focus on finding your true turnout muscles with the exercises in this section, but make sure you do one of the 'Piriformis Stretch Variations' often, so you don't get too tight! To stop the foot rolling in, remember the arch exercises from Stage 1 and practice plié in front of a mirror to strengthen the arch en fondu.

Losing Turnout

Losing turnout in the hips (if you find it hard to keep the hips square, or the foot turned out) is usually a combination weakness in your centre and not using your turnout muscles. Practice the 'Turnout Exercise in Kneeling' and 'Functional Turnout Exercise', and then repeat the knee bends, focusing on using the same muscles. Also practice the 'Side Lifts' to strengthen the core muscles.

Hip Dropping

If your muscles on the outside of your hip are not working correctly you will find it hard to keep the hips level when balancing on one leg, or en fondu. Practice standing on one leg and keeping the hips level by squeezing the side of the bottom you are standing on (rather than by lifting the other hip). Other work can be practiced by completing the 'Wall Press'.

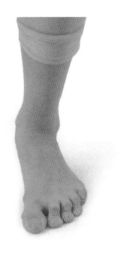

Clawing Toes

Your toes will claw if the weight is held too far back on the heel en fondu, or if the ankle joint is unstable and the extrinsic foot muscles are trying to grip the floor. Practice the 'Balance Exercises' from Stage 2 to help retrain the fine control of the muscles and ligaments around the ankle. Also, continue to work on the intrinsic strength of the toes with the 'Toe Swapping' and 'Doming' exercises. Practicing the 'Soleus Stretch' may also help stretch the calf and extrinsic foot muscles deep in the calf.

Stage 3 Exercises

Turnout Exercise in Kneeling

This is a great exercise to learn how to use your deep turnout muscles without using the bigger bottom muscles. You may not feel a strong contraction like you will with some other exercises, but just focus on keeping your hips still and isolating the rotating in your hip.

1. Start on your hands and knees, with your spine in neutral. Make sure your hands are squarely under your shoulders and your knees are under your hips.

2. Loop a resistance band around one ankle, and get a partner to stand on the other end, or fix it around a table leg. Slowly pull the foot in the band towards your supporting foot so that the shin is parallel with your other leg. Make sure that your hips remain square on and they do not move whilst performing the exercise.

3. Slowly and with control, move your foot back towards the beginning position making sure not to move your knee. The rotation of your leg should come from the deep turnout muscles under the hip. Practice this exercise 10 times on each leg and complete a total of two or three sets each side. Make sure that the back stays in neutral and your pelvis remains flat (do not tuck under.)

Checklist!
- Make sure that your back stays in a neutral position throughout the exercise.
- Keep your neck long and in line with your body.
- Keep your hands under your shoulders and your knees ubnder your hips.
- Keep both sides of your waist long.

Parallel to Turnout

This is a great way to feel your turnout muscles in action and there is no possibility of cheating! Your stomach muscles should be engaged at all times so you are not straining your back.

1. Lie flat on your stomach with your legs out straight. Your stomach muscles should be held so as to support your back. Shoulders are down and your head should be held gently without strain in the neck. Your arms should be in a comfortable position by your side or with your hands near your shoulders.

2. Lift both legs just off the floor in parallel. Remember to keep breathing and to keep your low back lengthened.

3. Slowly flex the feet, keeping the legs off the floor. Remember to keep your stomach muscles held and your shoulders down. There should be no strain in your lower back.

4. Turn your legs out, using your deep turnout muscles. Your feet should now be in first position and you will aim to hold this for three seconds.

5. Point the toes slowly, maintaining good turnout, keeping your shoulders relaxed.

6. Finally, lower the legs to the floor. Return the legs to parallel to begin again and repeat ten times.

Functional Turnout Exercise

Once you are aware of and can feel your turnout muscles working, try and use these as much as possible whilst in class. This is a great way to learn how to take the pressure off your thighs in a plié.

1. Stand with your back against a wall keeping your back in neutral and your body elongated. Have your feet in a wide second position making sure your feet as away from the wall slightly. Keep your spine in neutral (with a tiny curve in the low back) and keep your abdominal muscles on.

2. Slowly slide your back down the wall keeping your knees over your feet and your arches held into a wide plié. Place your hands behind your knees, and gently press the knees back into your palms. Hold this position for 3 – 5 seconds before slowly straightening the knees. Concentrate on keeping your turnout muscles engaged. As you return to the standing position be sure to pull up you inner thigh with your knee caps held ready for the next plié. Repeat this exercise at least ten times.

Checklist!
- Complete 2 – 3 sets and then perform the 'Piriformis Stretch' after each set of ten.
- Your lower back does not flatten and should have a small arch at the base of the spine.
- Remember to keep your stomach muscles engaged at all times. Keep your back upright and shoulders down.
- Feel the deep turnout muscles working behind the hips.

Piriformis Stretch

The piriformis is one of your biggest turnout muscles. This is a wonderful stretch for releasing tension deep in the back of the hips, and is perfect after any exercise focusing on turning out. It can also help with improving your flexibility for the splits and into turnout.

1. Lie on your back, with one leg stretched out straight. Bend the other knee up halfway towards your chest. Use the same hand as the bent knee to push the leg halfway across your body. Use the other hand to gently pull the shin of the lifted leg towards you.

2. You should feel a deep stretch in the bottom of the lifted leg. You should NOT feel pinching in the front of the hip. If you are feeling pain rather than a releasing stretch take care not to pull your knee in too far to your chest. Hold for 30 seconds, repeating twice each side.

Checklist!
- Make sure both sides of the pelvis stay in contact with the ground.
- The spine stays in neutral with the tail-bone on the ground.
- There should not be any pinching or pain in the front of the hip. If there is, do the 'Hip Flexor Stretch' in Stage 4 instead.

Tendu with Resistance Band

This is a great exercise to start working your inner thighs in the way that they are designed to work in class. When you first do this exercise, you can hold onto a barre or the wall. See if you can progress to doing it unsupported after a few weeks.

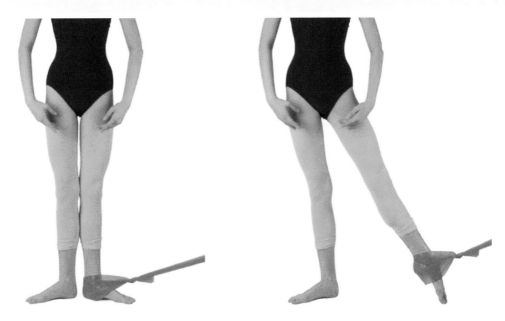

1. Stand in first position with a resistance band around one ankle. Ensure that it is attached to something heavy! Put your hands on your hips to check that they remain square. Engage your abdominals and turnout muscles to help keep your hips aligned.

2. Slowly tendu the working leg to second position, working through the demi-pointe. Use your inner thighs to close in first position against the resistance of the band.

Checklist!
- Make sure that your hips remain square to the front.
- Maintain turnout of the supporting leg.
- Keep your arches stay lifted at all times.
- Repeat at least 10 times on each leg.
- Make sure that your abdominal muscles are on throughout the exercise
- The body must stay upright, not leaning forwards or backwards, or to either side.

Single Leg Rises in Turnout

By now you should be pretty good at your single leg rises in parallel, so start practicing them in turnout. Make sure that everything stays aligned and that your fingers are resting gently on the bare, not gripping it.

1. Stand on one leg in a turned out position resting your finger tips gently on a wall or the barre. Hold the lifted leg in sur le cou-de-pied making sure the supporting foot is turned out and the arches in your foot are lifted.

2. Slowly rise up onto a full demi-pointe and then lower slowly. Repeat this exercise and many times as possible up to 20 times.

Checklist!
- Keep your chest lifted, with your spine in neutral and abdominal muscles on.
- Keep the lifted foot pointed at the ankle, with the thigh turned out from the hip.
- Toes remain long – no clawing!
- Rise to the full height of demi-pointe.
- Keep your weight centered between the first and second toes.
- The knee on your supporting leg remains pulled up throughout.
- Hips remain facing forward.
- Turnout of the foot is maintained as you lower the heel.
- Arches stay lifted at all times.
- At least 15 perfect rises.
- There should be no pain in the back of the ankle or big toe.
- The body must stay upright, not leaning forwards or backwards, or to either side.

Cat Stretch

This is a lovely way to warm up and gently begin moving the spine. There are many versions of this stretch and we have included the following exercise as it is very safe for almost everyone.

1. Start on your hands and knees keeping your spine in the neutral position. Your chest should remain open with your hands directly under your shoulders and knees under your hips. Keep your shoulders down your feet relaxed flat on the floor.

2. Breathe in filling your ribcage with air, arch your back and tuck your tailbone under. Roll through your spine curling it toward the ceiling. To continue the arch gently curls your head forward making sure to keep your neck relaxed. Your stomach muscles should be working creating an arch on the inside.

3. Now exhale releasing all the air from your ribcage and arch your back in the opposite direction starting by releasing your tailbone up to the ceiling. Remember to keep your shoulders down and your head and neck elongated. Be careful not to sink into your lower back. Repeat movements 2 and 3 at least six times, focusing on moving each bone in your spine.

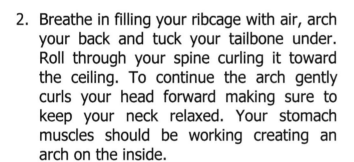

Checklist!
- Keep your neck long throughout, especially when you arch backwards.
- There should not be any pinching or pain in your back. Focus on moving each of the bones in order from your tailbone to your head.
- Keep your chest lifted away from the floor and your arms straight.

The Three Legged Cat Exercise

This exercise has two fantastic benefits by improving the strength of your buttock muscles and isolating the movement of your leg from your spine. Take it slowly at first and practice in front of a mirror so you are able to see exactly what is moving (or what isn't!).

Version I

1. Start on your hands and knees with your knees directly under your hips and your hands straight under your shoulders. Lift one leg so that the thigh is almost parallel to the floor whilst keeping the pelvis square and the knee bent to 90 degrees. Your partner can check that you spine is still in neutral.

2. Keeping your abdominals on and your knee bent, slowly push the heel up towards the ceiling. Be careful not to sink into the lower back and remember to hold your stomach muscles on. Lower the leg back down slightly keeping the knee bent and parallel to the floor. Perform 10 pulses of the leg before lowering that knee to the floor and repeating on the other side.

Checklist!
- Keep your lifted thigh parallel to the floor.
- Make sure to keep your stomach muscles engaged.
- Keep a small curve in your lower back throughout the exercise.
- Be careful not to arch and flatten you back while you move the leg.
- Keep your chest lifted away from the floor and your arms straight.

Wall Press

The muscle at the side of the hip (gluteus medius) helps keep the hips level when standing and balancing on one leg. It can be hard to train this muscle for its particular role however, this exercise does it perfectly.

1. Stand side on to a wall, as close as you can without twisting or shifting your ribcage and keeping both your knees slightly bent. Cross your arms over your chest keeping them out of the way. Lift the leg closest to the wall and bend your knee of the supporting leg whilst keeping both thighs in line. Make sure your back stays in a neutral position and hold your stomach muscles firm. Be careful not to let the hips tilt forward.

2. Press the outside of the knee of the lifted leg onto the wall, hold for 8 seconds. Make sure that your hips stay level, and you keep your stomach muscles engaged. Feel the muscle in the hip of the supporting leg working to keep the hips level.

Checklist!
- Do this three times in a row on each side (holding for 8 counts) then repeat the exercise twice on each side.
- Be sure to do the 'Gluteal Stretch' afterwards.
- Make sure to keep your stomach muscles engaged.
- Keep a small curve in your lower back throughout the exercise.

Gluteal Stretches

While we want our hips to be strong, it is also important that they stay nice and mobile. Remember to stretch out your gluteals after any strengthening exercises to prevent them from getting stiff.

1. Lie on your back, with the right foot crossed over the left knee. Reach your right hand through the window in your legs and hold your thigh with both hands. Make sure your lower back is resting comfortably on the floor. Gently pull the left thigh in towards your stomach. Remember to keep your spine in the neutral position and your deep stability muscles engaged. With your shoulders still relaxed and your head softly on the floor, hold this position for 10-30 seconds. Repeat this exercise on with the opposite leg.

2. Sitting on a chair keep your left foot flat on the floor with your knee bent to 90°. Lift the right leg and place the lower part of the shin bone across your left knee. Relax the right knee down, and make sure that both sitting bones are resting comfortably on the chair. Keep your back elongated and your shoulders down. Slowly lean the torso forward from the hips, keeping the back straight and you start to feel a gentle stretch. Hold the stretch for 30 seconds, release the right leg, and then repeat this exercise on with the left leg.

Checklist!
- Watch that you don't tuck the tail bone under, or curl the lower back when bending forward. This can put pressure on the lower back.
- This stretch should only be felt in the buttock of the top leg.
- When performing the exercise in lying, make sure to keep your tailbone on the floor.

Stage 3 Program

Day 1 is for testing and going through all the exercises slowly.
Days 2, 3, 5 and 6 you can do the exercises every day.

Exercise	How many?	Day 2	Day 3	Day 4	Day 5	Day 6
		Turnout	Turnout	Stage 1	Turnout	Turnout
Turnout Ex In Kneeling	2 x 10 reps			X		
Parallel To Turnout	2 x 10 reps			X		
Functional Turnout Ex	2 x 10 reps			X		
Piriformis Stretch	2 x 30 secs			X		
Tendu with Theraband	2 x 10 reps			X		
Single Leg Rises Turnout	10 reps/leg			X		
Cat Stretch	10 reps			X		
Three Legged Cat – V1	2 x 10 reps			X		
Wall Press	2 x 10 reps			X		
Gluteal Stretch	2 x 30 secs			X		

Day 4 is a rest day from the turnout exercises, but go back to the Stage 1 program to refresh your memory of the foot exercises.
Day 7 is a rest day.
Day 10 complete the Stage 1 exercises.

Exercise	How many?	Day 8	Day 9	Day 10	Day 11	Day 12
		Turnout	Turnout	Stage 1	Turnout	Turnout
Turnout Ex In Kneeling	3 x 10 reps			X		
Parallel To Turnout	3 x 10 reps			X		
Functional Turnout Ex	3 x 10 reps			X		
Piriformis Stretch	3 x 30 secs			X		
Tendu with Theraband	3 x 10 reps			X		
Single Leg Rises Turnout	20 reps/leg			X		
Cat Stretch	20 reps			X		
Three Legged Cat – V1	3 x 10 reps			X		
Wall Press	3 x 10 reps			X		
Gluteal Stretch	3 x 30 secs			X		

Day 13 is when to retest yourself!

Stage 4

Beyond The Barre!

We all know that we should only rest our hands lightly on the barre, however when it is there, we often place too much grip and this can make us look more stable than we actually are!

Testing yourself off the barre is the best way to see how much support you have been using with your upper body, and can help you find your true stability.

This section is all about learning to control your center using your deep core stability muscles, so that the rest of you can be beautiful and fluid. It will also help protect your back, which often can get a little tight and sore if you start en pointe when it is too weak.

Stage 4 Tests

The final stage, Stage 4, is about challenging your balance and stability without the support of the barre. Many girls rely on the barre too much and really struggle to do pointe work in the centre. Work on this now and you will find your pointe will be much easier.

Test	Weakness	Day 1	Day 13
Balance En Demi-Pointe *(page 79)*	Wobbling		
	Reduced height		
	Sickling in		
	Sickling out		
	Leaning back		
	Rolling arches on lowering		
Relevé Passé *(page 82)*	Poor demi-pointe		
	Wobbling		
	Sickling out		
	Not landing in fifth		
	Pulling back en demi-pointe		
	Bottom out on landing		

These exercises will be tricky if you haven't done the other stages properly so please don't be tempted to do the stages out of order! You need to have good range and strength in the feet before trying these so make sure all the other stages are completed and that you can do the tests easily.

Test 8
Balance on Demi–Pointe

1. Stand with your feet placed in first position with your hands on your hips. Take care with the placement of your feet, making sure that they are in a good tripod foot position and the arches are gently activated.

2. Slowly rise up onto demi-pointe on both feet making sure to keep your knees pulled up and your stomach held supporting your back. Remember to breath and shoulders down. Hold your balance for at least 5 seconds then slowly and with good control lower your heels back down into first position. Repeat this exercise 3 times.

Checklist!

- Try not to wobble on demi-pointe or pull the upper body back.
- Rise up to your full height of demi-pointe.
- The ankle must stay straight - no sickling in or out.
- Control both the rise and the lowering movements.
- Arches remain on both at the height of rise and as you lower your heels.

Common Problems with Balance on Demi-Pointe

Wobbling On Demi-pointe

It is very important to have strong muscles around your ankles before you start pointe work. Practice 'Rises with Theraband' this time with your hands on your hips to strengthen the muscles on the outside of the ankle. It is equally important to have very good control of the deep tummy and core muscles to control your balance when away from the barre., so do the 'Side Lifts' and 'Bug Legs' to improve this area. Single leg 'Demi-pointe Balances' at the barre will also help you find your centre

Sickling The Ankles Out

Sickling out happens if you are weak along the outside of the ankle. It puts you at risk of spraining your ankles and as the platform of a pointe shoe is very small, it is important to be able to stabilize your ankles before going onto pointe. Practice 'Single Leg Rises in Turnout' focusing on placing the weight between the first and second toes. You can also go back to the 'Seated Rises' exercise in Stage One to really check your alignment.

Rolling Arches on Lowering
To stop the arches rolling in as you lower the heel, remember to practice the 'Seated Rises' and perform your rises in front of a mirror again. All of the exercises such at 'Toe Swapping' and the 'Big Toe Exercise' will help to strengthen your arches. The biggest focus however must be made in class. As your turnout improves from the exercises in Stage Three, you should find it easier to keep your arches on when in class.

Reduced Height of Demi-pointe

By now you should have good range in your feet, so if reaching a full height of rise is still a problem, it will be either strength or balance issues that are holding you back. Work on your 'Single Leg Rises' in sets of ten, gradually increasing the amount you can achieve and practice the 'Demi-Pointe Balance' frequently to train the stability muscles in your ankles. If your range is still a problem, go back to all of the 'Foot Massage' in Stage One and see if you can improve your range a little more.

Pulling The Upper Body Back

This usually means that your stomach muscles are a little weak so extra focus is required on the 'Bug Legs' and 'Side Lifts' exercises in this section. When you do these, make sure not to arch your back. Practice your balancing exercises holding your finger tips gently on the barre in the beginning, then taking your fingers off for short periods of time. Focus on controlling the ankles, feet, turnout and abdominals in this position.

Clawing The Toes

You should be getting nice and strong in your feet by now, so do take care not to claw the toes when rising. If you are getting tight again unde rthe ball of the foot make sure to give your feet a good 'Foot Massage' at least twice a week to keep them nice and mobile. Also remember to keep your toes long when pointing the feet, as in the 'Pointe Through Demi-Pointe' exercise.

Test 9
Relevé Passé in the Centre

1. Start by standing in fifth position in the centre of the room holding your hands softly in bras bas (fifth en bas in Cecchetti). Make sure you shoulders are down and you spine elongated.

2. Slowly plié keeping your heels on the ground and then relevé bringing the front foot to a high retire position. Bring your arms up to first position remembering to keep your shoulders down.

3. Hold this position slightly before passing the lifted leg behind and landing in fifth position. Repeat this exercise 10 times, alternating your feet each time.

Checklist!
- Make sure you achieve a good demi-pointe position.
- The ankle must stay strong, no major wobbling.
- Land cleanly in fifth position of the feet each time.
- Both heels touch the ground with each landing.
- Body stays upright, not swinging forwards and backwards.
- Body stays upright, not swinging forwards and backwards.

Common Problems with Relevé Passé

Many of the problems associated with 'Relevé Passé in the Centre' are the same as for the 'Balance on Demi-Pointe'. Wobbling on demi-pointe, reduced height of demi-pointe, fishing or sickling the ankles and rolling the arches on lowering; can happen for all the same reasons. Practice the exercises explained on the previous pages to help with any of these issues.

Pulling the Upper Body Back

Try not to pull the body back when you relevé as it will throw you off balance and make the exercise harder than it really is! Try and keep your legs underneath you and the shoulders relaxed. Practice 'Side Lifts' and 'Bug Legs' to improve your strength your stomach and sides. When practicing relevé, focus on working the legs and abdominals while keeping your upper body relaxed. Remember, the more effortless it looks the better! Try with your hands on your hips instead, or practice the exercise side on to a mirror.

Not Landing On The Same Spot

If you find it hard to land on the same spot as you took off from, when doing relevé passé in the center, practice it at the barre first. Start slowly and then gradually progress to a faster pace as you get stronger. Work on your abdominal and side strength with 'Side Lifts' and 'Bug Legs' to help control the trunk further.

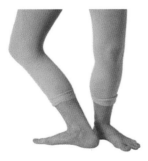

Not Landing In Fifth

Often dancers come down in some unusual foot positions when they land from a jump or a relevé. Make sure to land in a clean fifth position with the feet every time. Practice at the barre or in front of a mirror to watch your feet initially. This does take time, but makes a huge difference to your presentation when dancing.

Stage 4 Exercises

Piano Playing

Now this one will definitely take time to perfect! Being able to do this exercise is not a definite requirement before going onto pointe, but it will help improve the control of your toes a lot. It is often very hard to separate the second and third toes when you start this exercise. Keep working at it and you will be surprised how much you will improve. The more practice you do, the better you will get with these exercises. You can do them in your shoes, at school, waiting for the bus and while watching TV. Test the rest of your family and see if any of them can do this exercise.

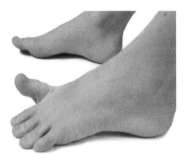 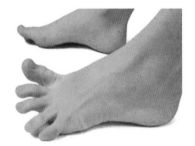 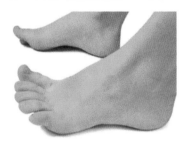

1. Set your feet up as for the toe swapping. Keep the ball of the foot flat on the floor throughout this exercise. Slowly lift the big toe off the floor keeping all of the other toes down.

2. One by one lift each of the other toes off the floor, keeping the ball of the foot flat on the floor. Make sure that the center of the heel is still engaged with the floor. Try not to roll the foot onto the outer edge.

3. Once all of the toes are lifted, start placing your toes back down on the floor starting with your little toe (pinkie) all the way through to your big toe. Make sure that the arches of your feet stay engaged and your foot does not roll in as you bring the big toe down to the floor.

Checklist!
- Use your hands to help your toes know where to go in the beginning.
- Using your hands alongside your feet can also help you make the right message in your brain to send to your feet.
- Do not give up! This one may take practice but it is very important!
- Make sure that the middle part of the foot does not roll in!

Tendus en Croix

Being able to correctly perform a Tendu is one of the most important skills in classical ballet from both a technique perspective and for injury prevention. Pay close attention to how you work the foot on the floor especially when working through the demi-pointe position before stretching the toes. It is important to practice this without ballet shoes on as it is amazing what you can hide inside a pair of ballet flats and even more so in a pair of demi-pointe shoes.

1. Stand in 5th with the right foot in the front and with your hands on your hips. Tendu the right foot forward to a demi pointe position, fully stretching the ankle.

2. Working the ball of the foot, as in the 'Doming' exercise, fully point the toes before closing the foot into fifth again. Do four slow tendus devant with the right foot, working through the demi-pointe. Then do 8 faster tendus smoothing out the demi-pointe transition yet still articulating the foot fully.

3. Repeat in a la seconde (4 slow tendus and 8 fast) and then to Derrière and then repeat with the left foot.

Checklist!
- Keep the supporting foot stable with arches on and the weight over the ball of the foot.
- Constantly focus on working through the demi-pointe of the working leg and keep your toes long and elongated.
- Practice keeping both legs turned out from the hips with hip bones facing the front at all times.
- Try to keep the middle joint of your big toe straight, pointing from the knuckle joint only.

Demi-Pointe Balance

It is a good idea to practice balancing on the demi-pointe position near the barre to find your centre of balance. Remember to keep your weight slightly forward, and lift up out of your centre. Using your abdominals and turnout muscles is the key to holding this position.

1. Stand facing the barre. Using the barre for support, place one foot onto demi-pointe and the other in a retiré or pirouette position. Find your balance, and hold the position by pulling up through the leg, and holding your abdominal muscles strongly. Feel energy pushing down the lower leg and into the floor and energy up and out the top of the head.

2. Slowly, take your hands off the barre and hold in first position (fifth en avant in Cecchetti). Balance for as long as you can, aiming for at least 5 seconds unsupported. Try and balance 5 times each side.

Checklist!
- Keep fully pulled up on your supporting leg
- Keep your deep abdominals on and your neck long.
- Keep your hips square to the front.
- Stay high on your demi pointe position.

Side Lifts

This is an excellent way to improve your core strength and is great if you tend to shift the ribs to one side when rising. To make it a little harder this time around, see if you can do the side lifts with your free hand on your hip instead of on the floor.

1. Start by lying on your side with your head resting on your arm (like a pillow). Place the free hand on your top hip, keeping your shoulder open. Make sure your feet are a little bit further forward than your hips. Gently contract your deep back and tummy muscles. Your back should be kept straight so that your waist should not be touching the floor.

2. Slowly, lift both legs just off the floor until your big toes are as high as your tummy button. Relax your shoulders (especially the top one) and breathe normally. Hold the legs off the floor for 5 seconds and repeat for 10 repetitions each side. If this is too hard in the beginning, start by lifting the top leg only and practice stabilizing in this position. Once you feel strong enough then try both legs at once.

Checklist!
- Make sure your underneath side (i.e. waist) is still pulled up off the floor and not touching.
- Keep your neck long and relaxed
- Try not to press down too hard with your hand into the floor.
- If you can do this easily, try kicking your legs in a little flutter kick while they are lifted off the floor.

Turnout Exercise in Retiré Position

This is a fantastic way to find your turnout muscles and learn to use them without anything else around the hips. Make sure you keep your tummy muscles on, and that your back and hips stay still.

1. Lie on your stomach with your legs in parallel. Bend one knee to 90° and take it out to the side slightly. Loop a resistance band around your ankle, and have the other end around a table leg or a friend's knee. Keep your hips in line (no hitching) and both hip bones on the floor. Have one hand under your forehead and the other under you hip to check for lifting of the hip.

2. Slowly bring the lifted foot towards the leg on the ground, as though you are going into a retiré position. Pause, then slowly release letting the leg come back to the starting position. Repeat ten times on one leg, keeping your hips still, repeat on the other side. Complete two sets of ten on each leg.

Checklist!
- Make sure you are using your deep turnout muscles and you are not gripping with the outer bottom muscles.
- Remember to release SLOWLY, so that you are working the muscles on the way up as well as the way down.

Piriformis Stretch

The piriformis is one of your biggest turnout muscles. This is a wonderful stretch for releasing tension deep in the back of the hips, and is perfect after any exercise focusing on turning out. It can also help with improving your flexibility for the splits and into turnout

1. Lie on your back, with one leg stretched out straight. Bend the other knee up halfway towards your chest. Use the same hand as the bent knee to push the leg halfway across your body. Use the other hand to gently pull the shin of the lifted leg towards you.

2. You should feel a deep stretch in the bottom of the lifted leg. You should NOT feel pinching in the front of the hip. If you are feeling pain rather than a releasing stretch take care not to pull your knee in too far to your chest. Hold for 30 seconds, repeating twice each side.

Checklist!
- Make sure both sides of the pelvis stay in contact with the ground.
- The spine stays in neutral with the tail-bone on the ground.
- There should not be any pinching or pain in the front of the hip. If there is, do the 'Hip Flexor Stretch' in Stage 4 instead.

Bug Legs (A)

This is a great way to improve the control of your abdominal muscles. You should not feel any strain in the back with this exercise and only take the legs out to a point where you are sure that the back is not moving and your stomach is well controlled.

1. Lie on your back and find a neutral spine position. Gently pull in your deep abdominal muscles, as though you are trying to hollow out the lowest part of your tummy, below your tummy button.

2. Slowly lift one knee up to 90°, making sure the back doesn't flatten or arch. Gently hold this knee with the fingertips of the same arm as the lifted leg. Make sure that the lowest part of your abdominals are still pulling in, not bracing out.

3. Lift the second leg to 90°, making sure that the tummy stays hollow and the back does not change position.

4. Lower the first leg back to the floor, followed slowly by the second leg, concentrating all the time on holding your deep tummy muscles engaged and your back in a neutral position.

Checklist!
- Make sure that you can keep breathing naturally and your shoulders are down.
- The spine stays in neutral with the tail-bone on the ground.
- There should be a tiny arch in the lower part of your back. However, your ribcage must be touching the floor.
- There should not be any pinching or pain in your back. If there is, just do one leg at a time until you can keep the deepest tummy muscles on.

Bug Legs (B)

Once you can maintain the tummy muscle contraction and back position whilst you are moving your legs, you can then progress to the next stage. This exercise is very easy to do incorrectly and very difficult to accomplish correctly, so make sure you read all of the instructions and progress slowly.

1. Start with both legs at a 90° and gently hold both knees with the fingertips keeping your shoulders on the floor.

2. Breathing out, slowly extend one leg to 45°, making sure that your back hasn't moved and your tummy is still hollowed. Remember to keep your shoulders down.

3. As you breathe in bring your legs back to the starting position and repeat the exercise on your other leg. Make sure that your spine is still in neutral and that your deep abdominals are still on.

4. Practice this exercise 10 times on each leg, remembering to breathe out as you extend the leg. As you get stronger, use less support through your fingertips, until you can do this exercise with your hands on the floor.

Checklist!
- Only do this version once you are confident with Version A.
- Make sure that you can keep breathing naturally and your shoulders stay relaxed throughout this exercise.
- The spine stays in neutral with the tail-bone on the ground.
- There should not be any pinching or pain in your back. If there is, go back to Version A for a little longer.

Hip Flexor Stretch

Often dancers get tight in the front of the hips and this can make it hard to turn out properly. This is a lovely stretch to open out the front of the hips, but make sure that you follow the instructions! Lots of people tip their hips forward in this stretch and wont feel it. The pelvis must stay upright.

1. Stand in a lunge position with your feet in parallel, facing forward ensuring both hips are square on. Gently bend the front leg keeping the back leg straight with your heel off the ground.

2. Slowly, bring the pelvis into neutral by pulling up through the deep abdominals and lengthening the lower back. Make sure you keep the upper body relaxed and centered over the hips.

3. Feel a gentle stretch in the front of the hip of the straight leg. If you do not feel a gently stretch try taking the leg further back. Hold for 10 – 30 seconds, repeating two to three times each side.

Checklist!
- Make sure you do not slump through the upper body or over extend the upper back.
- There should be no pain in the back with this stretch. Check the position of your spine if you feel any discomfort.
- Keep the weight forward over the front leg, and the back heel off the floor.
- If you find it difficult to balance, rest your finger tips gently on a wall. Work towards doing the stretch unsupported.

The Three Legged Cat Exercise

Some people find this version harder than Version I, and others find it easier! Always focus on keeping your back very still and isolate the leg movement from the hip socket. This will also help you build endurance in your upper body, which is an area where many dancers ar a little weak.

Version II

1. Start on hands and knees as for Version I, but with the working leg extended (in parallel) with the toe on the floor. Make sure that your arms are straight (but not hyper-extended in the elbows) and you hands are directly underneath your shoulders.

2. Slowly lift the leg until it is parallel with the floor. Make sure that the position of the spine does not change. Lower the toe back down to the floor and repeat ten times. Feel the gluteal muscles working on the way up and down. Do two or three sets of 10 lifts each side.

Checklist!
- Be sure to do a 'Gluteal Stretch' after each set.
- Take care to keep your chest lifted away from the floor and your neck long.
- Make sure that you do not 'sit' into the supporting hip.
- Get a friend to monitor the position of your back or watch yourself side on in a mirror.
- The spine should stay in neutral the entire time.

Stage 4 Program

Day 1 is for testing and going through all the exercises slowly.
On Days 2, 3, 5 and 6 you can do the exercises every day.

Exercise	How Many	Day 2	Day 3	Day 4	Day 5	Day 6
		Turnout	Turnout	Stage 2	Turnout	Turnout
Piano Playing	2 x 20 reps			XXX		
Tendu en Croix	8 slow, 16 fast			XXX		
Demi-Pointe Balance	20 secs			XXX		
Side Lifts	2 x 10 reps			XXX		
Turnout Ex In Retiré	2 x 10 reps			XXX		
Piriformis Stretch	2 x 30 reps			XXX		
Bug Legs (A)	2 x 10 reps			XXX		
Hip Flexor Stretch	2 x 30 secs			XXX		
Three Legged Cat V2	2 x 10 secs			XXX		

Day 4 is a rest day from the advanced exercises, but go back to the Stage 2 program to refresh your body on the foot exercises.
Day 7 is a rest day!
On Days 8, 9, 11 and 12 you do the advanced exercises.
On **Day 10** do Stage 2.

Exercise	How many?	Day 8	Day 9	Day 10	Day 11	Day 12
		Turnout	Turnout	Stage 2	Turnout	Turnout
Piano Playing	3 x 30 reps			XXX		
Tendu en Croix	8 slow, 16 fast			XXX		
Demi Pointe Balance	30 secs			XXX		
Side Lifts	3 x 10 secs			XXX		
Turnout Ex In Retiré	2 x 20 reps			XXX		
Piriformis Stretch	2 x 30 reps			XXX		
Bug Legs (A+B)	2 x 20 reps			XXX		
Hip Flexor Stretch	2 x 30 secs			XXX		
Three Legged Cat - V2	2 x 20 secs			XXX		

Day 13 is when to retest yourself!

Ongoing Program

You can of course keep going with any of these exercises once you are on pointe however, here is a sample of a program that you might like to follow practicing two or three times a week.

	Exercise	Repetitions
	Cat Stretch	**(10 times)**
	Bug Legs A + B	**(10 times each, each leg)**
	Side Lifts	**(10 times, 5 secs each side)**
	Three Legged Cat	**(10 times each leg)**
	Turnout Exercise in Retiré	**(10 times each leg)**
	Piriformis Stretch	**(2 times 30 secs each leg)**
	Piano Playing/Toe Swapping	**(20 times)**
	Single Leg Rises In Turnout	**(15 rises each side)**
	Rises With Theraband	**(10 times each side)**
	Calf Stretches	**(2 times, 30 secs each leg)**
	Pointe Stretch	**(2 times, 30 secs each foot)**
	Foot Massage	**(2 minutes each foot)**

Part 2

FAQs
About Pointe Work

Will it Hurt My Feet?

This is a really tricky question to answer. Yes, a lot of dancers do get pain in their feet when they do pointe work and there are lots of photos of horrible looking feet belonging to ex dancers, but this does not have to be the case!

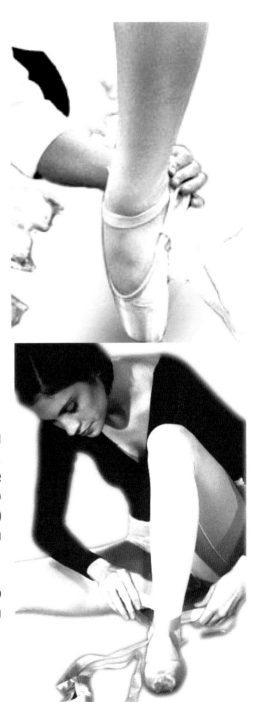

Most issues with pain are due to badly fitting shoes or weak feet, and it often happens when both are happening together! If you take the time to strengthen your feet well before starting en pointe and you get a shoe that fits your foot very well, you should have very little pain in the feet.

As dancers begin to do more and more hours en pointe, the chances of discomfort in the feet obviously increases but, you should be able to do several hours a week very comfortably. When you first start you will only do a few minutes at the end of each class.

If you are strong before starting pointe work, you can avoid taking strain through the growth plates. Most dancers have no issues at all with the growth of their feet and the problems that do occur (like stress fractures or ligament sprains) are usually because of bad technique or doing a step that is too hard for the dancer to control.

Many dancers have long careers with no problems with their feet. So the problem is not in doing pointe work, it is how you do it!

What Might Stop Me From Going onto Pointe?

Most of the problems and weaknesses that might stop you from progressing onto pointe can be fixed with specific exercises and hands on treatment such as massage and mobilization however, there are some things that may not be so easily fixed. It is very important that you do get checked by a specialist dance physiotherapist (physical therapist) or an experienced dance teacher before you start en pointe to notice these things.

Some issues that may stop you from going en pointe can include;

- Problems with the growth of the bones in your feet. Some people have problem areas in the bones of their feet from a previous injury that didn't heal correctly making the progression onto pointe difficult.

- A large Os Trigonum is a bone that a few people have at the back of the ankle and it can give you pain in this area. Obviously, when you go onto pointe this bone may squash the muscles around it and may cause irritation and pain. Many people can dance for years en pointe with one of these however if there is already pain behind the ankle, it may become more of an issue.

- Serious problems with the knees and chronic Patello-femoral pain (pain under the knee-cap) might hold you back a little however, with the correct strengthening exercises most of this will settle.

- A restriction in pointe range due to a bony foot rather than muscle or joint restriction may make it hard to progress onto pointe.

- Spinal problems, including severe scoliosis (sideways curves in the spine) or spondylolisthesis (slipping of one of the vertebrae in the lower back) could prove a problem if your back is unstable.

When Will I Know I am Ready?

Your dance teacher will be the one who really decides when it is time for you to think about moving onto pointe. They are the one that sees you dancing every week and they know all of your weaknesses better than anyone else. It is however, always a good idea to check with a dance physiotherapist (physical therapist) before starting pointe to asses all the small details to help you get onto pointe as easy as possible.

A good guideline for checking these details are:

- When you are doing 3 or more classes a week for at least a year.
- When you can achieve 20 single leg rises onto demi-pointe without adjusting your position halfway through.
- When you can do all the tests in this book with good control.
- When you have no injuries.

Remember, we all grow at different rates and we all have different strengths. The chances of all the girls in a class being ready to start pointe at the same time is fairly slim, so don't worry if there a few girls in your class that go onto pointe before you do. Just work on all the exercises given here and you will improve in strength remarkably.

Part 3

The Workbook

How to Use the Work Book!

Right, it's time to get to the real stuff! How much do we do, and how often? To tell you the truth, it doesn't really matter when in the day you do these exercises, as long as you do them. Place a copy of the chart up on the fridge or in your room to remind you to do them every day.

However, it does make it easier if you do these exercises at the same time every day. Maybe find time before or after school each day. Some people may find it easier to practice before dinner while others find they can always do them before bed. Whatever time you pick, do them every day and tick off each exercise as you go.

Give the feet a break from the 'Foot Massage' in the middle of the week. If you do too much too soon they might feel a little tender underneath. This is also a great exercise to test out on the family, especially if they have been on their feet all day, working, shopping or playing golf!

A two week program has been written for you to do for each section. Do the tests on day one and then again on day 13 and see just how much you have improved! If you can do the test very well it's time to move on to the next stage.

Practice the first day of a new stage on a day when you have a little more time (Sundays are usually good). Go through all the exercises for that stage slowly with the instructions so that when you do them during the week they are easily remembered.

If the tests are still a little difficult after two weeks of doing the exercises, it is quite acceptable to persist with that stage for a little longer until you feel you have achieved the correct requirements. The better you are at each stage, the better you will be en pointe!

Each stage works on a different area and the exercises will prove harder as you continue through. In the later stages, there are two days a week that you should review the exercises you did in the beginning to make sure that your feet remember how to do them!

These are all great exercises to keep going with when you move onto pointe. There is an ongoing day-by-day program at the end to continue making your feet and body stronger and stronger!

Stage 1 Tests

This stage is all about the flexibility in your ankles and feet. The more mobile they are, the easier it is to get right up onto your pointe shoes! Some people will find these tests easy than others and some may take a little longer to get there.

Day One:

Test	Weakness?	Day 1	Day 13
Demi-Pointe Range Test *(page 15)*	Reduced demi-pointe		
	Reduced pointe range		
	Toes clawing		
	Pain behind the ankle		
Pointe Range Test *(page 17)*	Reduced pointe range		
	Toes curling under		
	Ankles sickling in		
	Ankles sickling out		
	Knees bent		
	Pain behind the ankle		
Toe To Wall Test *(page 20)*	Heels lifting		
	Arches rolling		
	Less than 10cm		
	Pain at the front		

1. Go through the first three tests in the book and mark a cross in the box next to any weaknesses that you notice.

2. Go through all the exercises for this stage slowly with the full instructions so they are easy to remember.

Day 1 is for testing and going through all of the exercises properly.
Days 2 to 6 you can do the exercises every day.

Exercise	How many?	Day 2	Day 3	Day 4	Day 5	Day 6
The Tripod Foot	10x10 secs					
Calf Stretches	2 x 30 secs					
Pointe Stretch	3 x 10 secs					
Foot Massage	2 minutes			xxx		
Toe Swapping	20 reps					
Doming	20 reps					
Pointe Through Demi-Pointe	20 reps					
Seated Rises	20 reps					

Day 7 is a rest day!
Days 8 to 12 do more of the same exercises.

Exercise	How many?	Day 8	Day 9	Day 10	Day 11	Day 12
The Tripod Foot	20x10 secs					
Calf Stretches	2 x 30 secs					
Pointe Stretch	3 x 20 secs					
Foot Massage	3 minutes			xxx		
Toe Swapping	30 reps					
Doming	30 reps					
Pointe Through Demi-Pointe	30 reps					
Seated Rises	30 reps					

Day 13 Retest yourself! See if you have improved enough to go into the next stage. If so, "Congratulations!" If not, don't worry; just repeat the second week of exercises again until you can do all three tests really well. Remember, the more time and focus you put on these exercises the faster you will improve. But QUALITY is always more important than QUANTITY.

Stage 2 Tests

Stage 2 is about building strength in your feet and ankles so that you can cope with the constant demands of pointe work. The more you can focus on isolating all the little muscles in your feet the better! The more control you have of your intrinsic foot muscles before you start pointe work, the easier it is!

On Day 1 do the two tests and mark down which parts you have trouble with then, go over the exercises for that section. Follow the program on the next page for at least two weeks before retesting.

Test	Weakness	Day 1	Day 13
Single Leg Standing	Clawing toes		
(page 36)	Ankle rocking		
	Arches rolling		
	Big toe joint lifting		
	Gripping tendons		
	Hip hitching		
	Hip dropping		
Single Leg Rises	Leaning forward		
(page 40)	Clawing toes		
	Reduced demi-pointe height		
	Sickling out		
	Sickling in		
	Bending the knees		
	Losing turnout		
	Rolling arches		
	Unable to do 15 rises		
	Pain behind the ankle		

Remember to make sure you can perform the tests really well before moving onto the next stage. It doesn't matter if you spend three or four weeks on each stage as it will make the next stage a much easier process to go through.

Stage 2 Program

Day 1 is for testing and going through all the exercises slowly, to make sure that you are thinking of all the right things.

On Days 2 – 6 you can do the exercises every day.

Exercise	How many?	Day 2	Day 3	Day 4	Day 5	Day 6
Balance Exercises	10 x 10 secs					
Toe Swapping	20 reps					
Doming	10 reps					
Piano Playing	10 reps					
Pointe through Demi Pointe	20 reps					
Rises With Theraband	2 x 10 reps					
Single Leg Rises in Parallel	15 reps/leg					
Turnout Exercise In Retiré	2 x 10 reps					
Piriformis Stretch	2 x 30 secs					
Side Lifts	2 x 10 reps					

Day 7 is a rest day!

On Days 8 – 12 repeat the same exercises with just a little more in each sitting.

Exercise	How many?	Day 8	Day 9	Day 10	Day 11	Day 12
Balance Exercises	10 x 15 secs					
Toe Swapping	30 reps					
Doming	20 reps					
Piano Playing	20 reps					
Pointe through Demi Pointe	20 reps					
Rises With Theraband	2 x 10 reps					
Single Leg Rises in Parallel	20 reps/leg					
Turnout Exercise In Retiré	3 x 10 reps					
Piriformis Stretch	3 x 30 secs					
Side Lifts	3 x 10 reps					

Day 13 is when to retest yourself to see if you have improved enough to proceed to the next stage.

Stage 3 Tests

Stage 3 is about controlling turnout from the hips and building stability in the hips to help you balance en pointe. Focus on finding the deep turnout muscles with each of the turnout exercises and then try and use them in class!

Test	Weakness	Day 1	Day 13
Plié In First Position	Heels lifting		
(page 58)	Arches rolling		
	Big toe lifting		
	Toes clawing		
	Knees coming forward		
	Chest tilting forward		
	Bottom sticking out		
	Bottom tucking under		
	Unable to keep balance		
	Pain at the front		
	Uneven bend in knees		
Single Knee Bends	Body leaning forward		
(page 61)	Body leaning back		
	Hip hitching		
	Hip dropping		
	Toes clawing		
	Bottom tucking under		
	Bottom sticking out		
	Knee dropping in		
	Losing turnout		

If you can learn to use the correct muscles for turnout in class, you will help prevent a lot of injuries and will achieve a greater strength more quickly. Do not worry about losing flexibility as you get stronger. Having strong stable hips will actually help make you more flexible and will make stretching much easier.

Stage 3 Program

Day 1 is for testing and going through all the exercises slowly.
Days 2, 3, 5 and 6 you can do the exercises every day.

Exercise	How Many?	Day 2 Turnout	Day 3 Turnout	Day 4 Stage 1	Day 5 Turnout	Day 6 Turnout
Turnout Ex In Kneeling	2 x 10 reps			X		
Parallel To Turnout	2 x 10 reps			X		
Functional Turnout Ex	2 x 10 reps			X		
Piriformis Stretch	2 x 30 secs			X		
Tendu with Theraband	2 x 10 reps			X		
Single Leg Rises Turnout	10 reps/leg			X		
Cat Stretch	10 reps			X		
Three Legged Cat – V1	2 x 10 reps			X		
Wall Press	2 x 10 reps			X		
Gluteal Stretch	2 x 30 secs			X		

Day 4 is a rest day from the turnout exercises, but go back to the Stage 1 program to refresh your memory of the foot exercises.
Day 7 is a rest day.
Days 8, 9, 11 and 12 are for the turnout exercises.

Exercise	How many?	Day 8 Turnout	Day 9 Turnout	Day 10 Stage 1	Day 11 Turnout	Day 12 Turnout
Turnout Ex In Kneeling	3 x 10reps			X		
Parallel To Turnout	3 x 10 reps			X		
Functional Turnout Ex	3 x 10 reps			X		
Piriformis Stretch	3 x 30 secs			X		
Tendu with Theraband	3 x 10 reps			X		
Single Leg Rises Turnout	20 reps/leg			X		
Cat Stretch	20 reps			X		
Three Legged Cat – V1	3 x 10 reps			X		
Wall Press	3 x 10 reps			X		
Gluteal Stretch	3 x 30 secs			X		

Day 10 complete the Stage 1 exercises.
Day 13 is when to retest yourself!

Stage 4 Tests

The final stage, Stage 4, is about challenging your balance and stability without the support of the barre. Many girls rely on the barre too much and really struggle to do pointe work in the centre. Work on this now and you will find your pointe will be much easier.

Test	Weakness	Day 1	Day 13
Balance En Demi-Pointe	Wobbling		
(page 79)	Reduced height		
	Sickling in		
	Sickling out		
	Leaning back		
	Rolling arches on lowering		
Relevé Passé	Poor demi-pointe		
(page 82)	Wobbling		
	Sickling out		
	Not landing in fifth		
	Pulling back en demi-pointe		
	Bottom out on landing		

These exercises will be tricky if you haven't done the other stages properly so please don't be tempted to do the stages out of order! You need to have good range and strength in the feet before trying these so make sure all the other stages are completed and that you can do the tests easily.

Stage 4 Program

Day 1 is for testing and going through all the exercises slowly.
On Days 2, 3, 5 and 6 you can do the exercises every day.

Exercise	How Many?	Day 2	Day 3	Day 4	Day 5	Day 6
		Turnout	Turnout	Stage 2	Turnout	Turnout
Piano Playing	2 x 20 reps			XXX		
Tendu en Croix	4 slow, 8 fast			XXX		
Demi Pointe Balance	20 secs			XXX		
Side Lifts	2 x 10 reps			XXX		
Turnout Ex In Retiré	2 x 10 reps			XXX		
Piriformis Stretch	2 x 30 reps			XXX		
Bug Legs (A)	2 x 10 reps			XXX		
Hip Flexor Stretch	2 x 30 secs			XXX		
Three Legged Cat V2	2 x 10 secs			XXX		

Day 4 is a rest day from the advanced exercises, but go back to the Stage 2 program to refresh your body on the foot exercises.
Day 7 is a rest day!
On Days 8, 9, 11 and 12 you do the advanced exercises.
On **Day 10** do Stage 2.

Exercise	How many?	Day 8	Day 9	Day 10	Day 11	Day 12
		Turnout	Turnout	Stage 2	Turnout	Turnout
Piano Playing	2 x 30			XXX		
Tendu en Croix	8 slow, 16 fast			XXX		
Demi Pointe Balance	30 secs			XXX		
Side Lifts	3 x 10 reps			XXX		
Turnout Ex In Retiré	2 x 20 reps			XXX		
Piriformis Stretch	2 x 30 reps			XXX		
Bug Legs (A+B)	2 x 20 reps			XXX		
Hip Flexor Stretch	2 x 30 secs			XXX		
Three Legged Cat - V2	2 x 20 secs			XXX		

Day 13 is when to retest yourself!

Glossary – Ballet Terms

Battement Tendu (bat-MAHN than-DEW)
Tendu means to stretch. The working foot slides from the first or fifth position to the second or forth position, through the demi-pointe, without lifting the toe off the floor. Both knees must be kept straight. This movement results in a pointed foot.

Échappé (ay-sha-PAY)
Escaping or slipping movement. An échappé is a level opening of both feet from a closed to an open position.

Plié (plee-AY)
Bent, bending. Bending of the knee or knees. This movement is done with the legs turned out.

Relevé (ruhl-VAY)
Lifted or raised up. A movement in which the heels are raised off the floor.

Retiré (ruh-tee-RAY)
Withdrawn. A position in which the thigh is raised to the second position en l'air with the knee bent so that the pointed toe rests in front of, behind, or to the side of the supporting knee.

Sur le Cou-de-pied (sewr luh koo-duh-PYAY)
On the "neck" of the foot. The working foot is placed on the part of the leg between the base of the calf and the beginning of the ankle.

Acknowledgements

An enormous thank you has to go to my beautiful models, Antonia, Alice, Sophia and Kia who were so patient with me on a rather extended photo shoot!

These girls have been so beautifully trained that they all found it very strange to do all the 'bad' positions that I often see in initial pointe assessments!

All of these girls have been under my watchful eye as they prepared for (or are still preparing) for pointe. Antonia and Alice are just 11, Sophia is 12 and Kia has just turned 13.

A huge thank you also to all of my staff members who have patiently edited, and re-edited this book. It always amazes me how we can still find mistakes after so many revisions!

And finally to my partner Sarkis; Thank you so much for keeping me on track, for guiding me forward when it all felt too much, and for helping make my dream of sharing my knowledge with the world a reality. I don't think I would have made it without you!

All my love,
Lisa

Additional Resources

The Perfect Pointe System

'The Perfect Pointe System' takes the science of dance medicine off the text book and into the classroom! Enjoy the combination of anatomical and scientific research in a clear and easy to use format to transform your teaching of pointe work to young students.

The Perfect Pointe System encompasses not only a fabulous 130 page reference manual that provides formal assessment sheets and explains each test in detail, but also includes:

- **Wall charts** for easy reference.
- Details of **class plans** to provide integration of the course in to class work.
- Access to 30 weekly **audio recordings** discussing the finer points of each assessment test to further enhance understanding.

www.theteachersmanual.com

Parent's Manual

Many parents are bewildered by the whole experience that is the dance world and are often at a loss as to how best support their children, whether this is in regard to nutrition, training techniques or emotional coping strategies in times of stress.

This manual answers all of these questions and more, and best of all;

It's FREE!

I wanted to make sure that there was no barrier to any parent wherever they are in the world, no matter what the conversion rate is, to be able to access quality information that they can trust in regards to learning the best things for their children.

www.theperfectpointebook.com/TheParentsManual

The Front Splits Fast Flexibility Manual

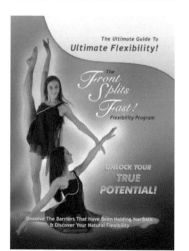

Getting into the splits comfortably is a dream for many dancers, as all dancers know flexibility is an important part of dance. 'The Front Splits Fast Flexibility Manual' will help you to reach your dreams!

It is a unique program that teaches you how to work with your body, not against it; To realize why it tightens up and all of the things that influence this; and to realize that most of the time, traditional stretching is the most inefficient way to get more flexible. Learn the secrets therapists have been using for years, to break through your flexibility barriers!

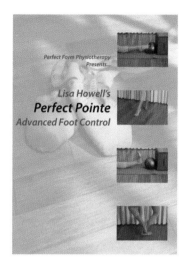

Advanced Foot Control

This course is specifically designed for more advanced students, professional dancers and dance teachers, to improve their knowledge and technique in regards to controlling their feet. 'Advanced Foot Control' goes into detailed explanations of the anatomy of your feet to teach you not only how the muscles in your feet work, but how you make your feet work better for you.

The manual also provides specific strengthening and massage techniques so that you can learn to self-treat. It is completely unique! Every time this course has been presented dancers and teachers have remarked that it has changed the way they view their feet completely.

Core Stability Course

There are many myths in the exercise and dance world about how to strengthen your core. This course will teach you the correct way of increasing your core stability in order to improve your dancing remarkably. It includes exercises to work on finding your natural spine, strengthen your inner and outer units as well as teach you how to activate your core when dancing! This course is essential for any dancer to discover the true secrets of core stability.

The Ballet Blog

In order to keep all of the information we have available to the public in one place on the internet, we have created a fantastic site that you can visit whenever you like.

There are loads of free articles, videos and frequently asked questions for you to browse through, as well as links to other dance articles and sites that you might be interested in..

If you would like to appear on the site, simply email us a photo and a short note about how this course has helped you with your dancing, and we will add you to our gallery.

For more information go to www.theballetblog.com

About The Author

Lisa Howell is a physiotherapist specializing in the education and treatment of dancers. She trained at Otago University in New Zealand, and after working in New Zealand, Australia and Austria, she has returned to Australia to fulfill her dream of sharing her fascination of the human body with the world. She owns and runs the Perfect Form Physiotherapy practice in North Sydney, New South Wales, Australia, and also lectures internationally to various ballet schools and sporting institutions on exercise rehabilitation and safe technique.

She has a close working relationship with several ballet schools; she treats injured dancers and performs pre-pointe assessments and screening tests to identify any possible issues as soon as possible. Sessions are often aimed at maximizing an individual's performance, rather than waiting for an injury to occur.

Lisa's aim is to develop a series of resources to allow dancers, athletes and the general public - wherever they are in the world – to have access to vital information that may change the way they work with their bodies. She enjoys working with athletes because of the responsibility they take for their own management, and their drive to achieve, or return to, full capacity as quickly as possible.

Lisa began dancing at the age of 5, doing both the RAD Syllabus and Flamenco dance. Throughout her professional studies and career she has continued her involvement with dance and uses her personal experience as a constant learning tool to advance her knowledge. She loves to have a close interaction with her clients, so please feel free to contact her through the open blog at www.theballetblog.com.

How to Order the Perfect Pointe Book

To order new copies of this book, simply log on to www.theperfectpointebook.com

This will take you to a page where you can leave your name and e-mail address. Do not worry, there is no chance of receiving spam emails by doing this. I respect your privacy and promise that your name and address will not be shared or sold to any other individual or company. It is purely so that you can receive the FREE Perfect Pointe Dancers Newsletter, with tips to help improve your dancing, and so that I can contact you with any new courses or publications regular updates that I am releasing.

From this page you will be directed to a web page that tells you all about the book. If you wish to purchase a downloadable copy simply click the link, and you will be taken to a checkout page where you enter your credit card details. This is a totally secure page.

After submitting your details and confirming payment, you will be forwarded to a page with all the details for downloading the book straight to your computer. I suggest saving it onto your hard-drive, and printing out a copy for easy use. Most girls get the printout bound at a copy store (about $5).

If you have any queries about the book or this process, please do not hesitate to e-mail me at info@perfectformphysio.com

I hope you enjoy the book as much as I did putting it together! Let me know how you go by posting an entry at www.theballetblog.com

Lisa Howell (B.Phty)

Made in the USA
Charleston, SC
09 July 2013